The Little
Bach Book

An eclectic Omnibus of *Notable Details*
about the *Life* and *Times* of the esteemed
and highly respected Johann Sebastian Bach

Humbly presented with most faithful
Scholarship and a ready *Wit*

David Gordon

LUCKY VALLEY PRESS
2017

Published by Lucky Valley Press
Jacksonville, Oregon
www.luckyvalleypress.com

Printed on acid-free paper   6.20

Dedication

During a formative and very intense 16-month period from April 1983 through July 1984, four conductors invited me to debut as tenor soloist with five different ensembles. I believe that without their generous encouragement back then, I would not have become acquainted with J. S. Bach, and this book might not exist. They taught me how to understand Bach's music.

Thomas Dunn
The Handel & Haydn Society
Boston, Massachusetts

Sandor Salgo
The Carmel Bach Festival
Carmel, California

Greg Funfgeld
The Bethlehem Bach Festival
Bethlehem, Pennsylvania

Helmuth Rilling
The Oregon Bach Festival
Eugene, Oregon
Die internationale Bach-Akademie
Stuttgart, Germany

Contents

Acknowledgements

Dale Moore was one of America's great voice teachers. I was 17 when we met, and he was 33. In two decades of voice lessons, the wisdom of his teaching enabled me to become a Bach tenor.

Barbara Bixby Gordon and I met as young adults and pursued a life of music together. Without her support, partnership and love, I would not have had a musical career and might never have encountered Bach.

Laurence Wasserman and Thea Dispeker were two of the finest artist representatives and best friends a singer could have. From our first meeting in 1980, they took me under their wing, guided my professional life, and opened doors for me all over the world.

In the summer of 1984 I met Hans-Joachim Schulze, Christoph Wolff, and the late Alfred Dürr for the first time. They were giving lectures and leading seminars at Helmuth Rilling's Internationale Bach-Akademie in Stuttgart and I was the new tenor soloist. I had the honor of listening to their presentations before our concerts—including a re-enactment of a Leipzig church service—and then the pleasure drinking wine and eating *Käsespätzle* with them afterwards. They have devoted their lives to studying Johann Sebastian Bach and his music, and fortunately for us they have produced many engaging and insightful books. Their writing and scholarship have inspired me for more than thirty years, and every lover of Bach's music is indebted to them.

For 25 years I have watched lecture audiences while they listen to me talk. In most cases I'm telling them about what they will hear in the concert hall in an hour or less, and my goal is to make them more eager to listen to the music and more open to connecting with it. Most of this book is based on material from my lectures about 18th-century composers and daily life.

After many early manuscript readers, my allies in the final pre-press months were the meticulous and dedicated proofreaders Susan Elliger and Ginna Gordon, to whom I owe many thanks. Any mistakes remaining are my fault, not theirs.

Special thanks to my St. Louis friends Steven Schenkel and Marcia Erwin, in whose peaceful guest room this book was actually completed.

Ginna Gordon supported *The Little Bach Book* from before its inception, and was a devoted proofreader and honest sounding board. She has experienced my serial enthusiasms for arcane and sometimes bizarre historical subjects with humor and an open mind. The food section is dedicated to her; we have actually tried the recipes on pages 50 and 51, and more. Ginna's love and encouragement enabled me to complete this project and I never could have done it without her. Thank you.

...his single concern was to create that which is true.

– Albert Schweitzer on Bach

INTRODUCTION

Johann Sebastian Bach (1685–1750) was a child of an era when music was transparent, complex, and elegantly structured, and he excelled in all of that, yet he also filled his music with powerful messages and vivid emotional expression. Bach created a balance of thoughts and feelings, mind and heart, and it is this combination of superb technical clarity and emotional reality that particularly distinguishes his music.

For several decades I've sung this music, taught it to singers, and talked with audiences about it, and I have noticed what kinds of stories, anecdotes, and explanations tend to engage their imagination. If we place the important names, facts and dates into a rich historical context we can often connect on a more personal level with the music and with the composer.

This book was created for that purpose. It places Bach and his life into the context of his era, using an eclectic and very personal selection of historical anecdotes, vintage illustrations, time lines, explanations, gee-whiz factoids, a bit of pathos, and lots of entertaining and completely true material about Bach and his world. Much of the source material was available only in German.

You can read from beginning to end or browse in any page order at all. The contents are intended to amuse, enlighten, educate and surprise. I hope these things are true for the novice as well as for the experienced Bach listener.

Bach led a type of life not often chronicled. He was neither royalty nor nobility nor a military hero. He wasn't particularly famous in his lifetime (except in the small world of professional musicians at his high level), and almost nobody wrote about him when he was alive.

Bach was not an independent "artist" in our modern sense. Musicians back then were either employees or impresarios. Bach was mostly the former and only a tiny bit of the latter. He was a salaried, middle class, business-savvy professional musician, and a mostly-unpublished composer. He was an employee his entire life, either as a musician in the court of a prince or duke, or as a salaried church musician paid by a City Council, and his career was a succession of jobs: Court, Church, Church, Court, Court, Church. That final Church job—in Leipzig from 1723 until his death in 1750—was by far the longest Bach ever lived in one place.

Leipzig was also the largest metropolis Bach ever lived in, and his demanding job kept him very busy and highly visible—he was a part of the vibrant cultural and religious life of a prosperous city of 30,000.

Because of the quality and quantity of Bach's musical work in Leipzig, because much of his activity there is well-documented, and because Leipzig itself is a window into the wider world around him, this book devotes most of its attention to Bach's Leipzig years.

Bach was a real person, not the marble bust on the music teacher's piano, or the crusty figure enshrouded in clichés. He worked hard every day and was the head of a large household living in an apartment in a big city. Every author of a book about Bach seeks in his or her own way to share a glimpse of that person. This book is my way.

– David Gordon
2017

Notes to the Reader:

1. Johann Sebastian Bach is the only person referred to in this book as simply "Bach." References to other Bachs always include first names, and the members of his immediate family are often referred to by first names only.

2. When writing about the music of Bach it is customary to include the BWV number with the titles. BWV stands for *Bach-Werke Verzeichnis*, or "Catalogue of Bach's Works." The BWV numbers provide a unique identifier for each of Bach's 1,128 compositions. Within the catalogue, the works are grouped by type (cantatas, concertos, organ, chamber music, etc.) and the BWV numbers do not represent the chronological order in which the pieces were written.

3. The spelling of German proper names in this book usually follows the prevailing usage in English for each person or place: the King of Prussia is more widely known in English as Frederick the Great than as Friedrich der Grosse. The Elector of Saxony is Frederick Augustus rather than Friedrich August.

On the other hand, English speakers almost always use German names when referring to members of the Bach family. (Johann Christoph Friedrich Bach is not John Christopher Frederick.)

Some language choices in these pages are based merely on personal preferences: for example the German spelling of Köthen, but the English spelling of Saxony. Other language choices are based on similar subjective factors, and my intention is simplicity and clarity.

4. Illustrations are derived from Public Domain images, stock photos, and from the author's own collection. See credits on page 139. All English translations are by the author.

Am Brunnen, vor dem Tore, da steht ein Lindenbaum.
(At the fountain by the gate there stands a linden tree.)

- Wilhelm Müller (1794-1827)

Prologue:

The Leipzig Inland Delta (*Leipziger Binnendelta*)

In a lowland region in eastern Germany about 100 miles southwest of Berlin lies the unusual confluence of three rivers: the Pleisse, Parthe, and White Elster. In olden days—before 19th-century engineers channeled and organized the meandering streams—the region was an enormous, ever-changing network of tributaries connecting the three rivers at their juncture. This inland delta was dotted with innumerable lakes and surrounded by dense forests and fertile land.

Geologists call this region the Leipzig Basin (*Leipziger Tieflandsbucht*). Archeologists have found evidence of human presence here as far back as 4000 BCE, and the oldest known settlements date back more than a millennium.

Most of the story in this book takes place in a prosperous town that grew in the middle of this ancient place.

The Settlement by the Linden Trees

700–900 CE: Slavic tribes from the east establish the first known settlements.

1015: A Slavic settlement is named after the Lipsk tree, known by Germans today as the *Lindenbaum*. In modern English it's known as lime tree, linden tree or basswood.

Over centuries the name evolves: Lipzk, Libzi, Lipzic, Leipsic, Leipzig.

1165: Leipzig is granted the right to hold public markets. The city is fortunate to be at the intersection of the Via Regia and Via Imperii, the two major trade routes from Norway to Rome and from Moscow to Spain.

1165: The original St. Nicholas Church is built, in Romanesque style. It was greatly remodeled in Baroque style in the 16th century.

1212: The St. Thomas Monastery is founded by monks of the Augustinian order. They also establish a school to educate boys and provide choristers for the Augustiner church.

1218: Merchants and craftsmen from other cities begin to settle in Leipzig.

1409: Leipzig University is founded, the second oldest in Germany after Heidelberg.

1481: Leipzig's first publisher opens. Printing will became a major Leipzig industry.

1496: On the site of their original chapel, the Augustiners construct the present-day St. Thomas Church.

1497: Leipzig's semi-annual trade fairs have become major regional events. The local economy is booming.

1539: The Protestant Reformation comes to Leipzig. The city closes the monasteries and destroys many of the buildings, but the churches are preserved. All formerly Catholic sanctuaries now become the property of the city, and the official religion is now Lutheranism.

Martin Luther preaches a celebratory Reformation sermon in St. Thomas Church on Pentecost Sunday.

Without interruption, the St. Thomas School choir continues to provide music for services at St. Thomas.

1618–1648: The Thirty Years War ravages Europe, and the human, economic, and environmental devastation are staggering. In three decades the population of Europe falls from sixteen million to fewer than six million.

(Bach was born only 35 years after the end of this war, when for the older generations it was still recent history.)

1626, 1636, 1643: During the war, three plague epidemics touch Leipzig.

1648: The Thirty Years War ends at last. Germany's small towns and rural areas are now subject to famine, hysteria, witch hunts, disease, and starvation. Leipzig's strength as a trade center helps it to survive.

1650: The world's first daily newspaper is published, the *Leipzig Einkommende Zeitungen (Coming Times).*

1680: The last and worst plague outbreak kills 2,200 Leipzig residents in five months—nearly 15% of the city's population.

1685: Johann Sebastian Bach is born in Eisenach, 120 miles west of Leipzig.

1687: The Leipzig Stock Exchange opens.

1693: The Leipzig Opera House opens, one of the oldest public opera houses in Europe. It never achieves the success of theaters in nearby Dresden or Berlin, and it closes in 1720, the victim of financial troubles.

1694: The Arabian Coffee Tree (*Zum arabischen Coffe Baum* [sic]), opens for business. It is Leipzig's first coffeehouse and one of the first in Germany.

1695: Zimmermann's coffeehouse opens on St. Catherine Street.

1700: Leipzig's population reaches 16,000, and will nearly double during the next three decades.

1701: The first streetlights are installed in Leipzig at intersections and on major buildings. 700 individual oil lamps are maintained by a regimented crew of lamplighters.

1702: Leipzig University student Georg Philipp Telemann founds a musicians' club (*Collegium Musicum*) for evening music-making at Zimmermann's coffeehouse. (Bach will lead this ensemble 1729–1740s.)

By the Early 1720s

Leipzig has become one of Europe's model cities, and one of the more expensive ones. It is the second city of Saxony (after Dresden), the center of the German printing and publishing industries, and an important European trading center.

The 25,000 residents enjoy a city of magnificent private dwellings. Its broad well-paved streets are illuminated at night.

There is a recently opened municipal library, a municipal water system feeding public fountains, a majestic town hall, a vibrant social life, and bustling trade and commerce.

Outside the massive town walls are elegant tree-lined boulevards and promenades and extensive formal gardens.

Leipzig's eight flourishing coffeehouses play an increasingly important role in the cultural and intellectual life of the city.

The university draws scholars and thinkers from far and wide, and the influx of visitors for the three annual trade fairs adds to the city's vibrancy.

A Deeply Lutheran City

Leipzig's eight churches offer an array of services weekly, most with music of some sort, and the major services at the two huge main churches include the most up-to-date choral/orchestral music.

The city's "Choral Music Director" oversees and directs the music in the main churches, teaches at the St. Thomas School, and provides music for weddings, funerals, and civic events of all kinds. It is an enormous job, and one that is becoming almost too much for one man to handle.

May, 1723

Leipzig's new Director of Music, Johann Sebastian Bach, arrives at the St. Thomas School with his wife, five children, and five wagons of possessions. Sebastian is 38 and Anna Magdalena is 22. They will spend the rest of their lives in Leipzig.

THE WESTERN WORLD IN 1723

Georg Ludwig, Prince-Elector of Hannover, is King George the First of Britain. He speaks no English.

Louis XV reaches maturity (age 13) and becomes King of France.

Prince Frederick—the future King Frederick the Great of Prussia—is 12.

Handel's opera *Ottone* premieres in London.

Mozart's father is 5.

There are thousands of coffeehouses in the cities of Europe—at least 1,000 in London alone.

In the colonies of the New World, more than 70,000 African slaves till the fields.

Benjamin Franklin, age 17, runs away from home and settles in Philadelphia to become a printer.

New Orleans becomes the capitol of Louisiana, a French colony claiming the middle third of the North American continent.

All these things were happening as Bach and his family arrived in Leipzig. What North Americans refer to as the "Colonial Era" is also the "Baroque Era" when referring to events in Europe. Communication and travel were slower, but then as now all things were interrelated and connected.

Bach the Employee

By the time Bach arrived in Leipzig in 1723, he had been a professional musician for two decades in a series of jobs: violinist in Weimar, organist in Arnstadt and Mühlhausen, and then back to Weimar as organist and third-in-command of the royal musicians.

In 1717 he had been offered his fifth job: the position of *Kapellmeister* for His Most Serene Highness Prince Leopold of Anhalt-Köthen. Kapellmeister (director of the court musicians) was the most enviable title a musician such as Bach could aspire to, and he agreed immediately—it was a big step up. However, he naively asked to be released from his Weimar obligations only *after* he had accepted the new job, and the Dukes of Weimar (two brothers) became mightily displeased and ignored him. When he persisted they threw Bach in jail for his insolence, but his new princely employer managed to get him out.

The Kapellmeister job in Köthen was ideal: the Prince was a singer and instrumentalist and performed in weekly house concerts alongside his superb ensemble of musicians. Bach had few church duties and therefore no amateur choir to deal with, just a life of music making with and for the Prince.

Then came the summer of 1720. Bach and Maria Barbara had been married for 13 years and had four young children. He left home in June to spend the summer at the royal spa of Carlsbad with the Prince and the courtly musicians and while he was gone, Maria Barbara died unexpectedly. (News was kept from him, and he learned of her death only when he returned home. See page 105.) During the next 18 months the grieving widower kept busy with his job, toyed with ideas of finding a new position elsewhere, and coped with being the father of four small children.

Bach occasionally wrote celebratory choral works in Köthen, but he had no resident singers there, so he hired out-of-town soloists when he needed them. Through this connection he met a young soprano named Anna Magdalena Wilcke, and they were married in December 1721. She was 20 and he was 36.

Only days after their wedding Prince Leopold also married, but his new bride had no affinity for Bach's compositions and she made the Prince's overall interest in music "somewhat lukewarm" (Bach's own words). Suddenly finding himself with little to do, the situation in Köthen became unsustainable. He was stuck in an isolated town far away from major cultural centers. He also had to think of his two sons; they would need a higher education and little Köthen had no university.

Toward the end of 1722, Bach learned that an important position had become vacant in Leipzig—a large city to the south in Saxony. It was not a Kapellmeister position, but one of the titles was *Director of Music* and that certainly had a good ring to it.

In reality it was mostly a school teacher/church musician job—and *he would have no organ or keyboard duties of any kind.* The base salary was modest, but housing was provided, there was a university for his sons, and there would be lots of opportunity for outside income in such a large city.

Bach wrote to Leipzig, but they put his application aside while they dealt with better-known candidates, some of whom had applied merely to leverage higher pay from their current employers. After the first applicants withdrew from consideration, the Leipzig City Council finally turned to the application from Kapellmeister Bach in Köthen. This memorable statement appears in the minutes of the council late that winter:

> *Since the best applicants are no longer available,*
> *less acceptable candidates must be considered.*

Bach traveled to Leipzig in early spring 1723 and auditioned for the city fathers by conducting the choir in two of his cantatas. They negotiated terms, and several theologians held a long meeting with Bach to examine his religious faith and principles. Finally, a lengthy contract was prepared and signed.

From the City Council's point of view Bach's primary duty was to serve on the teaching staff of the St. Thomas School and lead the choir of schoolboys in church services. From a letter seven years later to a good friend, it seems Bach originally may not have been entirely aware of the amount of school work expected of him, or just how uninterested the council members were in music.

His Leipzig job was one to which duties had been added over the decades without considering whether one man could manage it all. With his city contract, plus lots of sideline work, Bach was involved with some sort of public musical event virtually every day, either by necessity or by choice. His overall workload was probably heaviest in the early 1730s, and the following is a description of his six principal sources of income in those years:

Bach's Contract with the City of Leipzig

I. School Teacher (*Schulman*)

Bach was required to teach music and other subjects at the St. Thomas School. His ongoing stubborn ("incorrigible") resistance to classroom teaching—especially Latin—greatly exasperated the Leipzig City Council. After Bach died they explicitly sought a replacement who was more a teacher than a musician.

II. Choirmaster of St. Thomas (*Tomaskantor*)

Bach's contract obliged him to train the schoolboys in singing and musicianship and to rehearse and conduct them in church services, weddings and funerals. At any given time, Bach had around 55 choristers at his disposal, assigned as needed to duty in several churches where Bach oversaw the music. He repeatedly complained of the poor level of singers in his choir.

Boys' voices underwent the hormonal voice change at a later age in those days, and some sang soprano or alto in the choir until age 17 or 18. There is record of one boy who sang in the St. Thomas choir until his voice finally lowered when he was 23.

Bach personally oversaw the music in the St. Thomas and St. Nicholas churches, and provided a cantata with choir and instruments for the main Sunday service every week, alternating weekly between the two churches. On holidays and feast days, orchestra and choir were featured in both churches, one in the morning and the other in the afternoon, both led by Bach.

For these two churches between 1723 and the late 1730s, Bach wrote the *Magnificat*, four *Passions*, more than three hundred cantatas, at least nine choral motets, the *Christmas Oratorio*, and portions of the *Mass in B Minor*.

Christoph Wolff and other researchers estimate that Bach may have been involved in as many as 1,500 church services during his 27 years in Leipzig, performing each time to a capacity audience of 2,000 or more.

Under Bach's supervision, assistants led the music in two lesser churches: St. Peter and St. Matthew (known as the "New" Church). The music was minimal, perhaps a very small vocal group or just a few scholarship boys singing in unison to lead the hymns. (Bach was not involved with Leipzig's other (smaller) churches—St. John, St. Paul, St. George, and St. Jacob.)

III. Leipzig Director of Music (*Director Musices Lipsiensis*)

In his correspondence during the Leipzig years, Bach most often referred to himself as *Director Musices*. The city contract in effect made Bach the go-to person in Leipzig for music at weddings, funerals, public or official events, and royal visits. Although some of this was seen as part of his contractual duties, in most cases he received a separate fee.

OTHER FREELANCE MUSICAL WORK

Bach's base salary in Leipzig was 100 Thaler, but in a letter to a friend in 1730 he says his "income" is 700 Thaler. The difference came from city duties for which he was paid extra (including funerals and weddings), and from three areas of independent work unconnected to his city contract.

IV. Director of a Weekly Concert Series

From 1729 to 1741, Bach was the salaried conductor of the Collegium Musicum, a fine ensemble of university students and other local musicians. (He guest conducted frequently 1724–1729 prior to becoming director.) He either wrote, arranged, or obtained the music, and led weekly concerts at Zimmermann's coffeehouse in the winter and at Zimmermann's coffee garden outside the city walls during the summer months.

V. Private Keyboard Instructor

Bach's son Carl Philipp Emanuel recalled the family home as a "pigeon roost," a busy hub of activity with family and guests coming and going all the time.

Throughout his life, Bach was a dedicated and active teacher and mentor to his sons and his many private students. In fact, Bach had more private pupils than any other great composer. He began teaching in Arnstadt when he was 20, and during the next 45 years he taught at least 100 professional musicians, most of them organists.

By the time he arrived in Leipzig at age 38 he had established a reputation in Germany as a fine keyboardist, and out-of-town students were often present in the Bach residence. Bach gave room and board to students in return for their assistance in music copying and other helpful musical duties. They also had access to his music library and instruments.

Some of Bach's best-known keyboard compositions were instructional works intended for the development of technique—for example, the *Well-Tempered Clavier,* the *Two and Three Part Inventions,* and the series of *Little Organ Books (Orgelbüchlein)* were intended for students of all ages and levels. He was known for writing music to encourage his students to fully achieve a five-finger technique, with complete integration of the thumb into the fingering. Bach's pupils recalled that he gave them his own Inventions and Sinfonias as replacements for the existing (and less musically interesting) finger exercises and etudes used by other keyboard teachers at the time.

VI. Church Organ Examiner

When a church organ is renovated, or a new organ is installed, an accepted authority is hired to test the instrument and certify that the builder has fulfilled his contract and the organ is ready to be played (this practice continues in modern times). Such "examinations" were a lucrative sideline for Bach in towns throughout the entire region, and his resulting overnight absences from Leipzig were a source of displeasure for the City Council.

Bach conducted the examinations in the presence of the town authorities and the nervous organ builder. He began by "testing the lungs" of the organ, pulling out multiple stops and challenging the bellows to provide enough air. Then came a detailed evaluation of the keyboard, pedals and pipes, for which Bach improvised freely at the keyboards, letting his fingers follow his musical imagination. It must have been a memorable experience to hear Bach put a new pipe organ through its paces.

Opposite: The St. Thomas Church in a 1749 engraving by Joachim Ernst Sheffler. The St. Thomas School is the building at the far end of the plaza. From 1723 to 1750, the Bach family occupied all floors of the left end of the building.

The Two Main Churches (*die zwei Hauptkirchen*)

The churches of St. Thomas and St. Nicholas are not modest Baroque chapels: they are huge structures and have been the center of church life in Leipzig for more than eight centuries. In Bach's time the boys' choir from the St. Thomas School performed at both churches, and the services were usually filled to standing-room capacity.

The St. Thomas Church (*die Thomaskirche*)

The site was consecrated in the 12th century, and the first church was built in 1212. The current church was built in the 1490s in the late-Gothic style. In the 1890s, the interior was modified to reflect a 19th-century neo-gothic style, and ornaments were added to the exterior, especially the new portal in the formerly unadorned west facade.

The St. Thomas Church is the second largest in Leipzig, after St. Nicholas. The interior space is 164 feet long, 82 feet wide and 60 feet high. There was seating for nearly 2,200, and standing room for many more.

The St. Nicholas Church (*die Nikolaikirche*)

St. Nicholas is the largest church in Leipzig, and Bach actually spent more of his working time here than in St. Thomas.

A church was founded on this site in 1165, and the present church was built in the 1500s in a style known as a "hall church." The central nave and the two side aisles are the same height, and massive ornate columns support a huge expanse of ceiling over the entire space.

The interior is 207 feet long, 141 feet wide and 75 feet high. In Bach's time it seated as many as 2,400 worshipers, and many more could stand around the periphery. The interior of the church was extensively remodeled in the late 18th century, transforming it into something quite different from what Bach knew. Seating capacity in the church today is around 1,500.

The octagonal tower was begun in the 1500s and completed in 1730, in the midst of Bach's tenure. Another of Leipzig's famous fountains can be seen in the square.

Most of Leipzig's important or official liturgical events took place at St. Nicholas. It was the designated government venue for cantatas honoring the City Council or the Dresden Court, and for services of thanksgiving and allegiance to the Saxon rulers. There were curtained boxes for church and civil dignitaries and for Leipzig businessmen.

On May 30, 1723, Bach presented his inaugural cantata as Music Director in this church. Many other cantatas were premiered here as well as portions of the *Christmas Oratorio*. The *St. John Passion* was given its first performance here in 1724, and it was heard three more times at St. Nicholas during the following two decades.

A 20th-Century Postscript

After World War II, Leipzig found itself in East Germany behind the Iron Curtain, and beginning in 1982 peace rallies were held every Monday at St. Nicholas. During East Germany's "Glorious Revolution" in 1989, these Monday rallies became hugely important, and helped to ignite the peaceful uprising that brought about the fall of the Berlin Wall. The largest rally held in St. Nicholas during that time was attended by 8,000 people, an indication of the capacity of the sanctuary.

The events in 1989 are also a powerful testament to the place the St. Nicholas Church occupies in the hearts of the residents of Leipzig. Cabaret artist Bernd-Lutz Lange said about those Monday rallies:

> *There was no head of the revolution. The head was the St. Nicholas Church and the body was the center of the city. There was only one leadership: Monday, 5:00 pm, St. Nicholas Church.*

Above: The St. Nicholas Church in 1749. Engraving by Gabriel Bodenehr the Elder. *Below*: The St. Nicholas Church today.

Church life in Leipzig in the 1720s

When Johann Sebastian Bach arrived in Leipzig in 1723, it was a city of more than 20,000 in which church services were a living part of the fabric of daily life and a vivid expression of Lutheran faith.

Typical Church Schedule in Leipzig in 1727

The churches where Bach oversaw the music are shown in bold. Only events labeled as "services" included music. All services included a sermon, but not all services offered communion.

Sunday and Feast Day Mornings

5:00–6:00am - Matins service in **St. Nicholas** sung in Latin by ten choristers (recipients of city scholarships).

6:00–7:00am - Service in St. John.

7:00–11:00am - Services with communion in St. Jacob and the **New Church**.

7:00–11:00am - Services with communion at **St. Thomas or St. Nicholas** with a cantata for choir and instruments. The church with no cantata still had a service with communion. On special feast days, cantatas were heard in both churches—one in the morning and one in the afternoon, both led by Bach.

8:00–11:30am - Services in **St. Peter** and St. George.

9:00–Noon - Service at **St. Paul.**

11:30am–1:00pm - Midday service in either **St. Thomas or St. Nicholas** (alternated weekly). On major church holidays, services took place in both churches.

Afternoons on Sundays and Feast Days

2:00–4:00pm - Vesper service in **St. Thomas, St. Nicholas** and the **New Church.** The subject of the sermon is the Epistle for the following Sunday.

2:00pm - In **St. Peter,** a chapter of holy scripture was read.

2:00pm - Catechism exams in St. John.

3:15pm - Vesper service in St. Paul.

Monday through Saturday

6:30am - Early service at **St. Thomas** with communion.

2:00pm - At **St. Nicholas**, an hour of prayer and confessions.

2:00pm - Catechism and Bible exams in **St. Peter.**

2:00pm - At St. John, an hour of prayer and confessions.

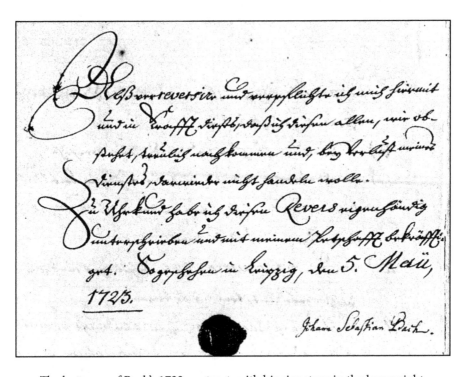

The last page of Bach's 1723 contract, with his signature in the lower right.

The Well-Tempered Title Page

Bach was a dedicated and influential music teacher. In 1722 he completed a collection of 48 instructional keyboard pieces, *Das wohltemperierte Klavier (The Well-Tempered Clavier)*. A decade later he wrote a second volume.

(Clavier is used generically in this context and simply means "keyboard.")

In each of these two volumes, Bach moves through all the 24 major and minor key signatures. Performing such a wide array of keys demands thoughtful tuning of the harpsichord or organ. Different key signatures call for slightly different shadings of instrument tuning but for the *Well-Tempered Clavier,* one tuning must suffice for all keys.

The distance between two notes varies almost imperceptibly according to the key signature. For example, the notes C and E occur in a C Major scale, and the interval between them is colored by their relative positions (1 and 3) in that scale. Both notes also appear in an A Minor scale, but their roles in the scale are different (3 and 5) and so is the distance between them.

The challenge is to tune the keyboard in such a way that C and E can sound good together in any key. To this end, there are many different methods of tuning a keyboard instrument. Bach knew this very well, and his title seems to imply that the music was written for "well-tempered" tuning rather than "meantone" tuning, the method used on most organs in his time. Nonetheless, his intention for the *Well-Tempered Clavier* is not clear, and the topic continues to be debated in musicological circles.

Like most of Bach's instructional music, these exercises also demand an agility of all ten fingers, including the thumbs. Thumb agility was not a new idea, but in Bach's complex keyboard music it was an unavoidable necessity.

On the following page is the title page of Bach's manuscript for Book I of the Well-Tempered Clavier. Scholars have long studied the whimsical swirling ornaments, and some interpret them as symbols and hints from Bach about tuning the instrument.

Opposite: The *Fugue in A-Flat Major* from Book II, BWV 886.

Das Wohltemperierte Clavier

The Well-Tempered Clavier, Book I, BWV 846–869

Title page of Bach's manuscript

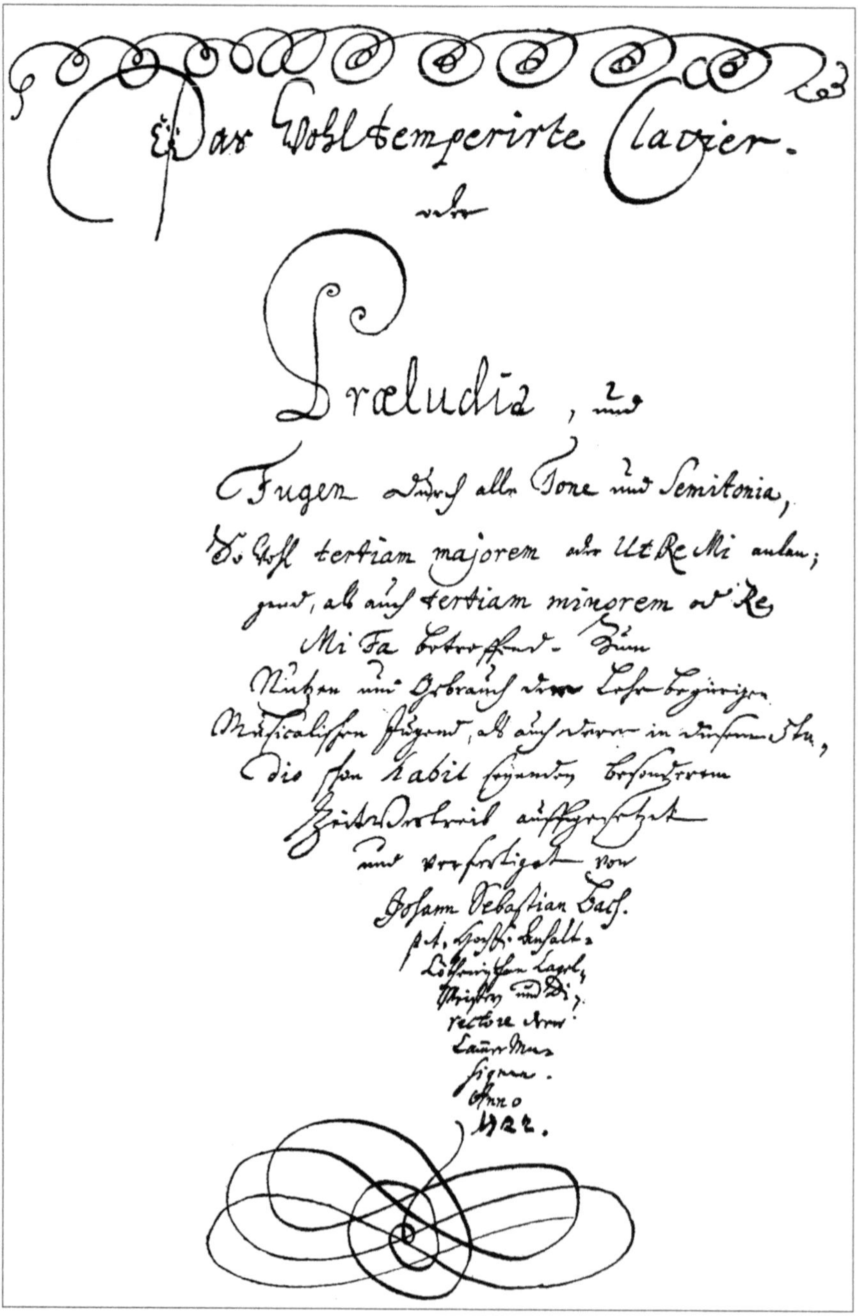
Das Wohltemperirte Clavier.
oder
Præludia, und
Fugen durch alle Tone und Semitonia,
So wohl tertiam majorem oder Ut Re Mi anlangend,
als auch tertiam minorem oder Re
Mi Fa betreffend. Zum
Nutzen und Gebrauch der Lehr-begierigen
Musicalischen Jugend, als auch derer in diesem studio
schon habil seyenden besonderem
ZeitVertreib auffgesetzet
und verfertiget von
Johann Sebastian Bach.
p.t: HochFürstl. Anhalt-
Cöthenischen Capel-
Meistern und Di-
rectore derer
Cammer Mu-
siquen.
Anno
1722.

Das wohltemperirte Clavier
oder
Præludia, und
Fugen durch alle Tone und Semitonia,
so wohl tertiam majorem oder Ut Re Mi anlan-
gend, als auch tertiam minorem oder Re
Mi Fa betreffend. Zum
Nutzen und Gebrauch der Lehrbegierigen
Musicalischen Jugend, als auch derer in diesem stu-
dio schon habil seyenden besonderem
Zeitvertreib auffgesetzet
und verfertiget von
Johann Sebastian Bach.
p. t: Hochfürstlich Anhalt-
Köthenischen Capel-
Meistern und Di-
rectore derer
Camer Musi-
quen.
Anno
1722.

The Well-Tempered Clavier,
or
preludes and
fugues through all the tones and semitones,
both the tertiam majorem or Do Re Mi [major]
and tertiam minorem or Re
Mi Fa [minor]. For
the profit and use of studious
musical youth, and also for those who are
already accomplished in this skill, for their
diversion, composed
and made by
Johann Sebastian Bach.
Currently Royal Anhalt-
Köthen Kappel-
meister and Dir-
ector of the
Chamber musi-
cians.
In the year
1722.

Brandenburg Concerto #3 in G Major, BWV 1048
Detail from the viola part

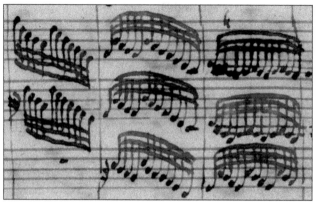

Christmas Oratorio, BWV 248
Detail from the first page of the full score

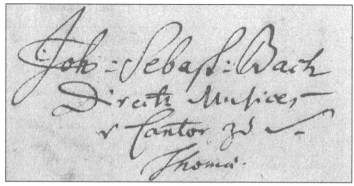

"Joh. Sebast. Bach
Director of Music
and Cantor of St.
Thomas"

Writing with a Feather

Writing in Bach's time was messy and time consuming. The enormous amount of letter-writing in those days is a testament to three things: 1.) there was no other way to communicate; 2.) human determination is amazing; and 3.) compared with our lives today, they didn't have much else competing for their attention.

It all had to do with feathers. Bach's *St. Matthew Passion* and the United States Constitution were written with feathers. So was everything else written with ink and paper until about 1810, when metal pen nibs first became available.

The image of someone writing with a big fancy peacock feather is a purely theatrical fiction. Quill pens were actually made of the very ordinary primary feathers of common birds, usually geese, but also crows, swans, and a few others—much less elegant than the theatrical version. For right-handed writers, the prized feathers were from the left wing, because those feathers tend to curve away from the face when held in the right hand.

Prepared quills could be bought in tied bundles from merchants in the city, but they were easy to make at home. The feathers were plucked and given a cursory cleaning. Often the barbs on one or both sides were completely trimmed, leaving

only the bare quill itself. The quills were then inserted into heated sand for a brief time to harden them. Then the exterior membrane was removed and the quill was cut into a typical pen nib with three basic strokes of the knife.

A quill was good for only 5 or 6 minutes of writing before the nib became soft and the quill had to be put aside to dry. After several such dryings, the tip of the nib needed to be trimmed slightly with a pen knife: not a folding knife, but a small razor-sharp blade on the end of a wooden handle. After several trimmings, the nib was recut from scratch. Only 3 or 4 nibs could be cut on a quill before it became too short to use.

Bach and the family members and assistants who helped copy his manuscripts and orchestra parts used enormous quantities of quills, and they would have had a routine for drying and trimming them.

Paper (*Papier*)

Paper was expensive, and was made in different forms and thicknesses for letters, contracts, music, etc. (For a composer or author in Bach's time, it was not unusual to write a new work on the blank reverse side of an older composition.)

Powdered pumice or sandarac, called pounce, was kept in a shaker, and sprinkled onto the paper to prepare the surface and to help keep the ink from spreading.

Bach did not use the more expensive pre-printed music-writing paper, which was a heavier stock than common paper; he used less-expensive blank paper and drew the staves on each sheet with a five-bladed device called a rastrum. This also enabled Bach to customize the layout of each page to suit the composition. His "fair copy" and presentation scores, such as the *St. Matthew Passion*, are beautiful, painstakingly created manuscripts.

Ink (*Tinte*)

Writing with a dip pen—even with a modern metal nib—is a difficult art. Controlling the ink flow is crucial, but early inks (often made from powder by the writer) were inconsistent and hard to manage, and took longer to dry.

Pounce, sand, and other absorbent substances were kept in another shaker and sprinkled onto the paper to dry the ink. (Blotting paper came into use in the mid-18th century). In some of Bach's manuscripts, traces of drying sand are still found in the folds. To help date old manuscripts, modern musicologists sometimes examine the grains of sand and compare them with sand found in other scores.

Bach's Writing Desk (*Schreibtisch*)

On the third floor of the renovated St. Thomas School building, the windows of Bach's composing studio looked to the west, over the Pleisse River. According to his son, Carl Philipp Emanuel, Bach composed at his desk and did not sit at the keyboard while writing music.

Simply by looking at Bach's Leipzig manuscripts, we can deduce what writing supplies he kept at his desk:

- a bundle of quills, trimmed and ready to use, and a place to dry soggy quills;
- a razor-sharp pen knife for trimming the quills and also for "erasing" mistakes by scraping the ink off the paper;
- black and red ink in pots, and powder to make more;
- single and double *rastrum*;
- a long straight ruler for drawing uniform vertical bar lines in orchestral scores;
- a shaker of sand and other substances for drying the ink.

German rastrum from the early 18th century.

This engraving by Georg Balthasar Probst was published in 1762, twelve years after Bach died. The west facade of the St. Thomas Church looms over the neighboring buildings. To the right of the church is the St. Thomas School.

Key to the detail above: **A.** The windows of Bach's composing studio. **B.** The Thomas Gate. **C.** Old city wall. **D.** Footbridge over the Pleisse River.

Home Life

Bach's Leipzig Neighborhood

Every day for 27 years, Bach walked across the St. Thomas courtyard shown on the facing page. The Bach family lived in a relatively spacious multi-floor apartment in the school building, and the free rent was a significant part of Bach's salary. The main fountain in the square is visible in both images. In the lower image a new fountain is shown closer to the school. Neither exists today.

Upper Illustration: 1723 copperplate by Johann Gottfried Krügner showing the school (to the left) and the church as they were when Bach arrived that year. A small group of black-robed choirboys is crossing the plaza. The fountain is visible near the lower right corner of the image.

For the first eight years the family had to put up with living in this rundown century-old building sorely in need of modernization. In 1731 they moved to temporary quarters while the St. Thomas School was extensively rebuilt.

Lower Illustration: Detail of a 1732 engraving by Johann Schreiber. In the background is the newly-rebuilt St. Thomas School. The church is barely visible on the right, and residential buildings are on the left. After the 1732 renovation, the formerly three-story apartment occupied five stories and had at least 1,800 square feet of floor space. The apartment occupied the left third of the building from ground floor to attic.

An architect's front elevation of the new school is shown on the following page. Also see the photograph on page 128. The school was demolished in 1902.

Bach and his family could come out the door, make a u-turn to their right, and walk away from us, down the Thomas Alley just to the left of the school. It leads to the Little Thomas Gate, a pedestrian portal through the massive city wall. Beyond the wall was the Pleisse River and tree-lined boulevards with businesses and outdoor restaurants.

The channels in the cobbled street surface were gutters for rain, human and animal waste, and other refuse. By the mid-1740s, most of the these open gutters had been replaced with underground conduits. See page 72 for more illustrations of these channels.

Heating (*Heizung*)

For many private homes, the open hearth was the heart of the house and provided most of the heat. The Bach household lived in a comparatively spacious multi-story apartment in a larger building, and so did not depend on one single heat source.

During the reconstruction of the St. Thomas School building in 1731, cast iron heating stoves were installed in several large rooms on four of the five floors of the apartment (including Bach's composing room on the third floor). The stoves were stoked from outer hallways, and the heated rooms themselves were smoke free.

On each floor, the smaller unheated rooms could be entered only through the heated rooms. Such heating stoves were coming into wider use and they were expensive. However, compared with an open hearth, they provided steadier, more efficient, and safer heat to a larger living area.

The official drawing of the renovated and rebuilt St. Thomas School after the re-opening in 1732. The Bach apartment occupied the left end of the building—three windows wide and five stories high plus double attic. The front door of the apartment is in the lower left between the two ground floor windows.

Clothing (*Kleider*)

The clothing of the middle class was simple in construction. Cotton was expensive and rare, and a cotton thread strong enough for sewing had not been developed yet, so most fabrics were made of linen, wool, or silk.

The most commonly used German word for "underwear" is *Unterwäsche* (literally *under laundry*). The shirts, underskirts, and underclothing of the Bach family would have been white linen. It was much easier to wash than silk or wool, and the whiteness of the visible portions of one's linenwear was an important status symbol.

The outer clothing—vests, trousers, jackets, dresses, gowns, cloaks, capes— were kept superficially as clean as possible, but could not be laundered.

In the 18th century, women wore a long shirt, cotton stockings, and possibly an underskirt (*Unterrock*). Women's dresses were a multi-layered affair of linen, silk, and wool.

Men first put on a long-sleeve collared shirt of white linen that extended to mid-thigh and was sometimes tied together between the legs, making it take the place of undershorts. Neither men nor women wore separate undershorts until the early 19th century.

Trousers were buckled below the knee and worn with cotton leggings. Over the shirt and trousers was a long vest buttoned in the front and tightened with laces in the back. Various styles of long jackets were worn, with the white shirt collar and cuffs proudly visible.

The 1908 Bach statue at the St. Thomas Church. See page 114.

The Laundry (*die Wäsche*)

In most middle-class households in the early 18th century, doing the laundry involved several days of work and took place only a few times each year. A general average was three to five washings annually—even the wealthy did not put on a clean shirt every day.

For most people, especially in less urban settings, "laundry day" actually lasted nearly a week, and required preparation and planning.

If a household could afford it, a wash maid was hired and paid a laborer's wage for a few days. Moneyed families had their own wash house or shed, the lower middle class might share in the work or share a public structure. The laundry had to be inventoried and all the white items were counted to make sure none had been lost or stolen by servants.

After the sorting, the actual laundering begins:

Day 1:
Fine and colored items are soaked in lukewarm soapy water. Dirtier and sturdier items are soaked in water to which lye has been added.

Day 2:
Spots are treated by rubbing with soap, but sparingly, because soap is expensive. The fine items are transferred to a tub of plain water so that the soap does not dry on them before Day 3. Then the coarse items, which had been soaking in lye water, are transferred to the soapy water in which the fine items had been soaking.

Days 3 and 4:
The laundry is rinsed in lukewarm or cold water and hung out to dry. Ironing continues throughout Days 3 and 4. The iron is heated in proximity to fire, and has to be regularly re-heated, but not too hot, or it would burn the fabrics.

After ironing, the laundry was carefully folded, sorted, and stored in a laundry cabinet for safe keeping.

When the Bach family moved back into their apartment in the newly-rebuilt St. Thomas School in 1732, there was a new laundry room on a lower level at the rear of the building. It had a large built-in copper washbasin, a modern feature at that time. The Bach laundry room may have had its own supply of cold water from the fountain in the plaza, but the water still had to be heated by fire, probably in the kitchen on the second floor. Nonetheless, an indoor laundry room was a modern improvement, and no doubt made it convenient for Anna Magdalena and her helper or housekeeper to do laundry more often.

The Bed (*das Bett*)

The evolution of the modern bed began in the middle ages with the appearance of the canopy bed—a place to sit during the day, and a sleeping alcove surrounded by curtains at night.

Early mattresses were simply a linen or cotton bag filled with feathers, straw, wool and/or cotton and sewn shut. The fabric, called ticking, needed to be closely-woven, and often it was waxed or rubbed with soap to help keep it impenetrable. Because they were just bags with no inner structure, mattresses needed shaking and re-shaping every day. Fluffing and plumping the mattress was one of the arts of housekeeping.

By the early 1700s, the feather or eiderdown comforter (*Federbett*) was in wide use, and people slept on top of the feather-stuffed comforters as well as under them. The best featherbeds were filled with a high proportion of down; larger feathers needed to have their quills clipped.

Mattresses and wool blankets were aired as often as possible. The linen bedding was changed infrequently.

First and Second Sleep (*erster und zweiter Schlaf*)

Before the 19th century, people did not sleep the night through; sleep was divided into two distinct shifts. The practice was universal and unremarkable, and so it is rarely mentioned in contemporary letters other than passing references to *after first sleep* or *before second sleep.*

Household illumination was messy, inadequate, and dangerous, and most people went to bed no later than an hour or two after sundown. They slept for several hours, and then woke up—this was first sleep. Then they spent an hour or two in prayer, thought, conversation, or sex, depending on the bed partner, or they might monitor the coals in the kitchen hearth or in an enclosed heating stove. Finally one fell asleep again and entered second sleep which lasted until morning.

Whatever happened in the bedroom between first and second sleep usually took place in the dark because it was considered irresponsible and dangerous to read in bed and risk falling asleep with a light burning. The bedroom was the place in the home where house fires most often started, and a fragment of candle wick or a sputter from a sapwood strip could ignite the bedding in seconds.

In the 19th century, sleep habits were changed by the increasing availability (and safety) of artificial illumination in and outside the house. People could choose to stay up later and be productive during the evening hours. The industrial revolution also brought about a change in sleep habits: for employees who worked 12 hours or more, sleep had to happen in one shift, not two.

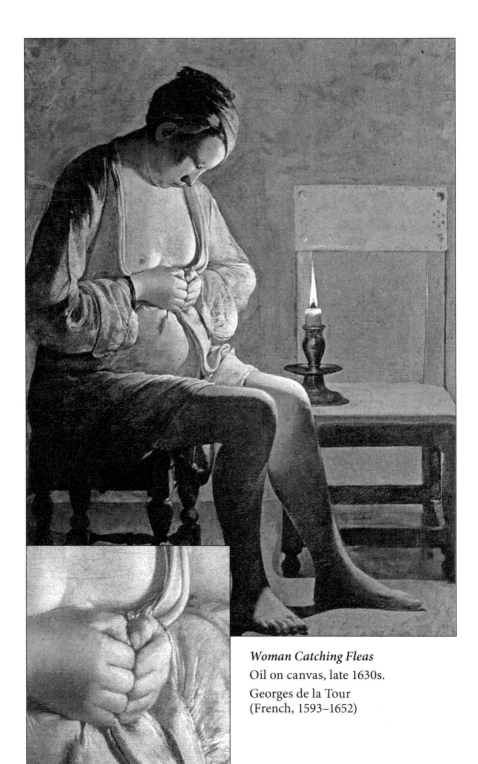

Woman Catching Fleas
Oil on canvas, late 1630s.
Georges de la Tour
(French, 1593–1652)

Fleas (*Flöhe*)

Pests and parasites were common in Bach's time, but fleas were especially widespread and well-known by everyone.

British author Isaac Disraeli (1766–1848, the father of British Prime Minister Benjamin Disraeli) published his book *Domestic Anecdotes of the French Nation* in 1794. In it, under the heading "Singular Frivolity of the Adulative Courtiers," he tells the story of a scene at the Palace of Versailles:

> *In the summer of 1775 the queen [Marie Antoinette] being dressed in a brown lutestring [a dress of plain, glossy silk], the King [Louis XVI] good humouredly observed it was "couleur de puce," the colour of a flea, and instantly every lady wanted to be drest in a lutestring of a flea colour. The mania was caught by the men, and the [fabric] dyers in vain exhausted themselves to supply the hourly demand.*
>
> *They distinguished between an old and a young flea and they subdivided even the shades of the body of this insect; the belly, the back, the thigh and the head were all marked by varying shades of this colour. This prevailing tint promised to be the fashion of the winter.*
>
> *The venders of silk found that it would be pernicious to their trade, they therefore presented new satins to her majesty, who, having chosen one of a grey ash colour, Monsieur exclaimed that it was the colour of her majesty's hair! Immediately the fleas ceased to be favourites and all were eager to be drest in the colour of her majesty's hair.*

King Louis might also have been referring to the bloodstains on bedsheets after a flea has been crushed. In any event, the point here is that an 18th-century French king living in one of Europe's greatest palaces was familiar enough with fleas to knowingly joke about their color, and if Louis XVI knew about fleas, so did everyone else. Every night before getting into bed people checked themselves and each other for fleas, just as the young woman in the painting is doing.

Once found, a flea had to be immediately killed. The woman in the painting is crushing a flea between her thumbnails.

Many people tried to be proactive with tiny flea traps, carved from ivory, wood, or coquilla nut, to be worn around the neck, carried in a pocket, or placed in a linen chest. A sticky substance like honey (and maybe a drop of blood) was placed in the trap, and the fleas entered through the intricate holes and got stuck.

Such a trap is unlikely to have made much difference, but it must have been satisfying to check your traps once in a while and see that you have caught a few.

Hairstyles (*Frisuren*)

Women's Hairstyles

The illustration on the cover of this book, engraved in 1710 or so, shows women on the streets of Leipzig wearing the then-popular Fontange hairstyle. The Fontange craze passed, the sheer height of hairstyles declined, and low, more natural hairdos came into fashion by 1720.

Middle and upper-class women often wore their own hair in elaborate styles rather than a wig. Most used no hair powder, in order to show off the natural beauty of their hair. Also, powdering one's own hair significantly increased the difficulty of keeping it clean (see below).

Men's Hairstyles

Men were clean shaven and facial hair was not in fashion, except in the military. For ease of care, many men kept their hair cut very short and wore wigs. Even small towns had wig-makers and there was a wide variety of wig styles.

Wigs (*Perücken*)

A good wig was made of human hair of any color, and was not necessarily white or powdered. Wig powder was a combination of starches like potato, wheat, or rice flour, plus coloring pigments if applicable, and fragrant oils. Of course the perfumed hair powder also served as one more source of general odor control.

A clean face, clean hands, white shirt cuffs, and a freshly powdered and perfumed wig meant that a man was "clean" regardless of all other evidence to the contrary.

The tidy and formal oil paintings of the day conceal the serious messiness of a powdered wig. First, a pomade was applied to the hair so that the powder would adhere, and thus powdered wigs were not actually dry and dusty, but rather oily and sticky.

Many men wore the tail of their wig tied in a small silk or linen bag at the base of their neck to prevent oil stains on the shirt and jacket collar, sometimes visible on original 18th century jackets.

Hair Washing (*das Haarwaschen*)

Most people did not shampoo with water, and both men and women used dry shampoo. Ingredients such as clay, wheat flour and other powdery substances were heated gently in a dry pan to remove every possible bit of moisture. At bedtime the powder was worked into the hair, in the night it bonded with the oils and dirt, and in the morning it was combed out.

Fashion and Prestige (*Mode und Ansehen*)

The portraits below and on the following pages show twenty different wigs. With the exception of Scarlatti, all the men below were Germans, and all were active in the early 1700s.

Domenico Scarlatti

Johann Kuhnau, Bach's predecessor in Leipzig

Johann Adolfe Hasse, Dresden Opera Director

Johann Heinrich Ernesti, St. Thomas School Rector

George Frideric Handel

Georg Philipp Telemann

Gottfried Reiche, Bach's principal trumpeter

Christian Ludwig, Margrave of Brandenburg

Johann August Ernesti, St. Thomas School Rector

The Bach Family (*die Bach'sche Familie*)

In 1730, Bach and Anna Magdalena had been living in Leipzig for seven years and their family was growing. They had produced seven children of their own in nine years, and three had survived. Four children from Bach's first marriage also were living in the apartment.

In October, Bach wrote a letter to his old friend Georg Erdman and included a description of his family:

> *I am married for the second time, my late wife having died in Köthen. From the first marriage I have three sons and one daughter living... From the second marriage I have one son and two daughters living...*
>
> *The children of my second marriage are still small, the eldest, a boy, is six years old. They are all born musicians, and I can already form vocal and instrumental ensembles within my family, especially since my wife sings a good clear soprano, and my eldest daughter also joins in not badly.*

(The complete letter is shown on page 79.)

Bach's son Carl Philipp Emanuel provided information to his father's first biographer, Nikolas Forkel, including this mention of Bach's domestic life:

> *In his life my father did not really make what could be considered a brilliant success in the world. On the one hand, he had a secure job, but on the other he had a great number of children to support and to educate on his income. If he had thought to travel and promote himself, he would have received the admiration of the whole world. But he was too occupied with his work and his art to think of pursuing ways which, perhaps, would have led to a gold mine. He loved the quiet domestic life, constant, uninterrupted occupation with his music, and he was a man of few needs.*

On the opposite and following pages are images of Bach and his four musician sons. They are the only members of the Bach family for whom we have portraits.

Portraits on the opposite page:

Top left: Bach as Concert Master in Weimar c.1715. Authenticity uncertain.

Top right: Bach as Kapellmeister in Köthen, c.1720. Authenticity uncertain.

Lower: The only portrait of Bach known to be authentic. It was painted in 1746 by Elias Gottlob Haussmann, official painter to the Leipzig City Council.

This 1733 painting is believed by some to show J.S. Bach and three of his sons, although the authenticity is not certain. The four subjects are holding (left to right) cello, violin, flute, and violin. In the lower right corner is a folding music stand on the corner of the table. (As a point of reference, the ages of Bach's sons in 1733 were: Wilhelm Friedemann 22, Carl Philipp Emanuel 19, Johann Gottfried Bernhardt 18, Gottfried Heinrich 9, and Johann Christoph Friedrich 1.)

WILHELM FRIEDEMANN BACH
b. November 22, 1710, Weimar
d. July 1, 1784, Berlin

Son of Bach and Maria Barbara. He was 13 when the family moved to Leipzig, and he attended the St. Thomas School, as did his younger brother and two half brothers. A renowned organist, he began his career at the St. Sophia Church in Dresden and then became organist at the Liebfrauenkirche in Halle. Friedemann was a virtuoso who found it difficult to succeed in church and court settings, and he left his Halle job and lived his final years in relative poverty.

CARL PHILIPP EMANUEL BACH
b. March 8, 1714, Köthen
d. December 14, 1788, Berlin

Son of Bach and Maria Barbara. Known as Emanuel, he was the most successful of the composer sons. He spent part of his career in Berlin as keyboardist for Frederick the Great, and then moved to Hamburg and succeeded his godfather Georg Philipp Telemann as Kapellmeister. (Emanuel received the name "Philipp" in honor of Telemann.)

JOHANN CHRISTOPH FRIEDRICH BACH
b. June 21, 1732, Leipzig
d. January 26, 1795, Bückeburg

Son of Bach and Anna Magdalena. Just before his 18th birthday he was appointed harpsichordist to the court of Bückeburg and subsequently became Concert Master. (The title signifies a leadership position rather than first violin in the orchestra.). He served in Bückeburg his entire life.

JOHANN CHRISTIAN BACH
b. September 5, 1735, Leipzig
d. January 1, 1782, London

Son of Bach and Anna Magdalena. Known in the family as "Christel," he was 15 when his father died. He first went to live with his half brother Carl in Berlin, then spent some time working in Italy, and finally settled in London, where he was known as John Bach. For a brief time there he was a teacher of the young Mozart.

The 1733 pastels of Wilhelm Friedemann and Carl Philipp Emanuel are attributed to Gottlieb Friedrich Bach (see page 112), Leipzig, c.1720. The portrait of Johann Christoph Friedrich is by Georg David Matthieu, Bückeburg, 1774. The oil painting of Johann Christian is by Thomas Gainsborough, London, 1776.

THE 23 BACHS

Johann Sebastian Bach had twenty children: seven with Maria Barbara and thirteen with Anna Magdalena.

Note that ten of these children died before reaching the age of five. One son died of illness at age 24, and another was mentally disabled. Of the remaining children, four sons had careers as professional musicians and one daughter married. Three daughters remained unmarried, and as a result lived their adult lives in relative poverty.

Maria Barbara (née Bach)
October 20, 1684–July 7, 1720
Married October 17, 1707

1. Catharina Dorothea (unmarried)
   December 29, 1708–January 14, 1774

2. Wilhelm Friedemann (composer)
   November 22, 1710–July 1, 1784

   Twins:
3. Johann Christoph
   February 23, 1713–died at birth

4. Maria Sophia
   February 23, 1713–March 15, 1713

5. Carl Philipp Emanuel (composer)
   March 8, 1714–December 14, 1788, Berlin

6. Johann Gottfried Bernhard (organist)
   May 11, 1715–May 27, 1739

7. Leopold Augustus
   November 15, 1718–September 29, 1719

Anna Magdalena (née Wilcke)
September 22, 1701–February 22, 1760
Married December 3, 1721

8. Christiana Sophia Henrietta
   Spring 1723–June 29, 1726

9. Gottfried Heinrich (mentally disabled)
   February 27, 1724–February 12, 1763

10. Christian Gottlieb
    April 14, 1725–September 21, 1728

11. Elisabeth Juliana Friderica
    April 5, 1726–August 24, 1781
    ("Liesl" "Liesschen")
    *In January 1749, Liesschen married one of her father's
    pupils, organist Johann Christoph Altnikol. The very
    strong-willed young woman in the Coffee Cantata was
    named Liesschen. That work was composed by her father
    when she was eight or nine years old.*

12. Ernestus Andreas
    October 30, 1727–November 1, 1727

13. Regina Johanna
    October 10, 1728–April 25, 1733

14. Christiana Benedicta
    January 1, 1730–January 4, 1730

15. Christiana Dorothea
    March 18, 1731–August 31, 1732

16. Johann Christoph Friedrich (composer)
    June 21, 1732–January 26, 1795

17. Johann August Abraham
    November 5, 1733–November 6, 1733

18. Johann Christian (composer)
    September 5, 1735–January 1, 1782

19. Johanna Carolina
    October 30, 1737–August 16, 1781 (unmarried)

20. Regina Susanna
    February 22, 1742–December 14, 1809 (unmarried)

Anonymous early 18th-century Dutch engraving showing the kitchen of a manor house or inn. A pot hangs over an open fire, roasting spits hang ready to use, and racks or grates allow food and pots to be placed over the fire. Preserved meats and strings of garlic and onions hang from the ceiling. A chain mechanism turns the meat roasting spit, a tray catches the drippings, and a ladle is used to baste the meat. Cookbooks were as popular then as now, and that might be a recipe book on the table.

FOOD AND DRINK (*Speise und Getränk*)

THE KITCHEN (*die Küche*)

Managing a household in the 18th-century household was a difficult and labor-intense job. Most kitchen conveniences we rely on today had not yet been invented. There was no refrigeration of any kind—except a cool room in the basement—and maintaining a store of supplies required careful planning.

As in most multi-level dwellings of that time, the kitchen and main living room in the Bach apartment were on what Americans call the 2nd floor (that is, up one flight of stairs from the ground floor; the Germans call it the 1st floor). The kitchen had no running water. A pantry on the first floor was used as a staging area, and kegs or buckets of beer were kept in a cooling room on a lower level. Foodstuffs, buckets of water, and arm loads of firewood had to be carried up a flight of stairs to the kitchen, the garbage was carried back down and discarded, and the waste water was poured into a pipe in the kitchen that drained into a gutter running past the south end of the school, through the city wall, and into the river.

Leipzig's Fountains (*die Leipziger Brunnen*)

Leipzig had abundant sources of water from the surrounding rivers and from wells and artesian springs, and attempts began in the early 1500s to create a municipal water system. By the time Bach arrived in Leipzig in 1723, several dozen impressive public fountains supplied water to the neighborhoods within the city walls. The fountains were fed by a network of underground pipes, and many were magnificent sculpted works of art. *Contemporary accounts indicate that people did not drink this water unboiled in the early decades of the century; it was used for cooking and washing.*

The daily operation of these fountains was essential to the community. Each fountain was tended by a member of the neighborhood paid to maintain the fountain and keep it clean and functioning. Some fountains required drawing water up from a cistern with a bucket, and the ever-present fountain warden assisted. He also kept the *Schleife* prepared—a sled bearing a large water container, ready to be dragged by its ropes to the site of a fire.

Water for daily use was carried in buckets from the fountain to the house, a tedious and never-ending job. Residents who could afford it hired a *Wasserzieher* (*water bringer*) who filled the buckets and carried them to the home.

Bach's Leipzig apartment was renovated in 1731, at a time when the city was experimenting with the installation of water pipes from the municipal system to the ground floor or inner courtyard of certain large homes or buildings. It is unclear if the Bach apartment had such a water line but if it did, it would have been a feature of urban modernity enjoyed by only a few lucky city dwellers.

FIRE (*Feuer*)

Cooking always involved an open fire fueled by wood. Not until mid century did a fully-enclosed cookstove appear with places on its top for multiple pots and pans. (It was invented by a Frenchman in 1735.)

Until then an open hearth was where all cooking took place: food was boiled, stewed, roasted, fried, poached, steamed, simmered, and grilled. An array of brackets, chains, pulleys, hand-turned rotary spits, and racks and trivets of all sizes enabled the cook to place the food, pots, and kettles over the heat.

By the mid 1600s masonry stoves were coming into use—square fireboxes 2 to 4 feet on each side and stoked with firewood through an open portal in the front. One large hole in the center of the top allowed heat and smoke to escape from the box, and pots were hung over that hole. The entire concept was tamer and safer than an open hearth, but it still involved cooking over a wood fire.

The kitchen was one of the deadliest rooms in the house. For 18th-century middle-class women, fire was the leading cause of accidental death—greasy aprons, sputtering fat, and open flames were a constant hazard.

An enclosed firebox, used for cooking. The fire is stoked through the low portal, pots are suspended over the large hole in the top, and the smoke escapes into the flue over the box. See page 43.

Beverages (*Getränke*)

Water (*Wasser*)

In 18th-century Europe, water was a beverage of absolute last resort. Rivers and groundwater were often polluted with human and animal waste, and most people chose to go thirsty rather than risk serious illness by drinking plain water.

Other non-alcoholic beverages existed, although none could satisfy a person's daily need for hydration. Safe beverages included dairy products, almond milk, and drinks made with boiled water such as herbal and black teas, and coffee. Coffee substitutes were made using roasted chicory or barley. (Coffee and coffeehouses are discussed on page 85.)

Beer (*Bier*)

Beer was the primary daily beverage for people of all ages in both urban and rural areas. The brewing process eliminates the pathogens in the water, and the alcohol content in the beer discourages harmful bacteria for a while, so the beverage is safe to drink. It was consumed at every meal and was also used in cooking (see recipe below). The alcohol content was much lower than modern beer, and it was often further diluted at home.

People bought beer at taverns and breweries—within the walled city of Leipzig in the 1720s there was one tavern for every 75 residents. Beer was either brought home in buckets or purchased in barrels and stored in a cooling cellar (the 1732 renovation of Bach's apartment added a cooling cellar for beer).

Bach and Beer - three vignettes

When Bach returned to Weimar in 1708, his annual salary was 150 florins in cash, eighteen bushels of wheat, twelve bushels of barley, four cords of firewood, and thirty buckets of beer.

Bach made a trip to Halle, in 1713, at age 28. His bill for a two-week stay at the Inn of the Golden Ring included 18 groschen for beer, enough to buy 32 quarts, an average of 2.3 quarts per day. His bill also included brandy, tobacco, and snuff.

Bach's contract in Leipzig 1723-1750 entitled him to a refund of the excise tax he paid on beer—up to three barrels annually—and receipts exist in the city records showing that Bach took full advantage of this. A barrel was 95 gallons (360 liters), and so the Bach family received a tax refund for nearly 300 gallons of beer annually. At first glance that might seem like a lot, but there were often a dozen or more residents in the Bach apartment, and less than one gallon per day for the entire household was actually very little. The Bach family consumed beer far beyond the three-barrel refund limit.

> *Wer kein Bier hat, hat nichts zu trinken.*
> *(He who has no beer has nothing to drink.)*
>
> – Martin Luther

THIRSTY STUDENTS

An example of the consumption of beer by young people is given in Anton Weiss's book, *Verbessertes Leipzig, (Improved Leipzig)* published in 1728.

In 1701, the City Council of Leipzig had a new cellar built under the St. Thomas School to store barrels of beer for the students. At that time the school had no regular supply of beer, and on hot summer days the students either went thirsty or drank from jugs of water kept in the dormitory. But that water was often contaminated by rats, and illnesses resulted. A sympathetic donor's heart was moved by the sight of the "languishing" thirsty pupils, and he provided funds to supply the boys with plenty of beer and pay for the construction of the beer cellar under the school.

In 1702 the same donor also purchased a mug (*Krug*) for each of the 55 students. That year a new statute was added to the school regulations stipulating that for the main meal on Sunday each pupil would be given one *Nösel* of Leipzig beer. That's about 1.25 pint, or 0.6 Liter. For the rest of the week the pupils could consume as much *Kofent* as they wanted—a weak, low-alcohol beer.

Early 18th-century German ceramic beer mug (*Krug*) with a pewter lid.

WINE (*Wein*)

Germany's largest and most famous wine-growing regions are found in valleys in the southwest, hundreds of miles from Leipzig. The two small wine regions closest to Leipzig are the northern-most vineyards in Germany, and grapes have been cultivated there for nearly nine centuries.

The only wine appellation (*Anbaugebiet*) located in Saxony is a small area close to Dresden in the valley of the Elbe River, about 75 miles from Leipzig. It's the smallest and eastern-most appellation in Germany.

The other appellation near Leipzig is in the neighboring province of Hesse, in the Unstrut and Saale River valleys near Freyburg and Naumburg.

No matter where it came from, wine was more expensive than beer, and although widely enjoyed, it was not used as a substitute for drinking water.

German Foods in the Early 1700s

Food as a Class Symbol

The whiteness of the bread on your table was a symbol of your level of prosperity in the world. Early German cookbooks distinguish between the simpler *Bauernspeise* ("farmer" or "peasant" food) and the more refined *Herrenspeise* ("gentleman" food), and bread is a good example of this. Brown bread was made from coarser, unrefined flour, and was considered peasant food. White bread, on the other hand, was made from refined and more expensive white flour, so it was a gentleman food.

Bread (*Brot*)

After the Thirty Years War, the second half of the 1600s began with traumatic hunger and famine, especially in the landlocked areas of Europe. Vast areas of cropland had been destroyed, grain shortages were acute, and flour and bread were foods of the wealthy.

By 1690, bread had reappeared as a significant, stand-alone item in the middle-class diet, usually made from wheat, barley and oats, and less commonly from millet and spelt. For all baked goods, yeast was the only leavening agent; baking powder and baking soda had not been developed yet.

The Boy with the Sausage Spit, a mid-century engraving by Daniel Nikolaus Chodowiecki showing a boy turning a spit over a firebox.

Meat and Fowl (*Fleisch und Geflügel*)

By the beginning of the 18th century, meat, fowl and fish had returned to the middle-class table after the scarcities following the Thirty Years War. As the land healed and agriculture was re-established, beef, pork, veal, mutton, and all kinds of fowl became available once again.

The most likely animal proteins on Bach's table would have been chicken, pork or mutton, cooked in every manner possible over an open hearth: stewed, simmered, roasted, grilled, or fried. Veal was the most expensive meat, fine beef was hard to find, and both were mostly foods of the well-to-do.

Also, because dairy foods were so important to the diet, much of the livestock and grazing land was devoted to producing milk rather than beef.

When slaughtering and butchering animals, every possible iota was made into some sort of food. Internal organs, intestines, brains, ears, tongues, lips, feet, marrow, blood, and all other bits were cooked, dried, salted, smoked, pickled, or made into a variety of sausages.

Fish (*Fisch*)

Ocean fish were always available in the coastal cities, but in landlocked cities like Leipzig, only fresh-water fish and preserved fish were on the table. Fresh salmon, pike, perch, and eel were luxury foods, although prices dropped during seasonal surpluses.

More affordable river fish included lamprey, sturgeon, and especially trout and other smaller fish. *Krebs* (fresh-water crayfish) were a very popular menu item, either eaten whole or made into soup, mousse, or even strudel. Salt-preserved herring and cod (*Stockfisch*) from the North Sea were sold at the Leipzig market, especially during Lent.

Eggs and Milk (*Eier und Milch*)

Eggs and dairy products were available year-round, and were an important source of protein. Eggs (quite smaller than modern eggs) were frequently used to thicken soups and bind ingredients.

Since milk spoiled quickly without refrigeration, it was supplied from dairy farms on the outskirts of Leipzig and sold at the market daily.

The most common home uses of milk were to make butter, clarified butter (*Milchschmalz*), sour cream, and *Quark*—a homemade "farmer's cheese" similar to cottage cheese, made by straining curdled sour milk through cheesecloth. Surprisingly, hard cheeses were not as popular then as they are today.

Eggs are used in three of the four sample recipes shown on pages 50–51.

Potato (*Kartoffel*)

Sixteenth-century Spanish explorers brought the potato to Europe from Peru, Bolivia, Colombia, and Ecuador around 1600, and it became an important addition to the northern European diet: it could survive long periods of cold weather, and because it's a root crop it was less subject to destruction by looting armies. In the early 1700s German cookbooks began to include potato recipes, and by mid-century the potato was being consumed in most of Europe. (Imported rice was available, but was used more for soups or sweet recipes like rice pudding.)

Vegetables (*Gemüse*)

Other local vegetables included turnips, parsnips, rutabagas, carrots, onions, leeks, broad beans, green peas, broccoli, and cauliflower. Vegetables were significantly smaller (and less visually perfect) than their modern counterparts. See the salad ingredients below for more vegetables available in the 1700s.

Tomatoes were introduced to Europe in the 1600s, but they were thought to be poisonous and were grown only as ornamental plants. By the 1720s, they had just begun to show up in Italian cookbooks (as a spicy sauce), but were not yet being eaten in Germany.

Salad (*Salat*)

Often thought of as a relatively modern invention, salads actually had become a major part of meals throughout Europe by the 16th century. They are included in cookbooks and are usually recommended as a warm-weather dish.

According to seasonal availability, salads were made from lettuce, wild greens, endive, artichokes, cress, celery, apples, radishes, onions, fennel, fresh and pickled cucumbers, dried and green beans, seed sprouts, beetroot, chicory, asparagus, and flowers.

Cabbage (*Kraut, Kohl*)

White, red, and savoy cabbages were eaten and prepared in many ways, but white cabbage was especially valuable when preserved as sauerkraut, a dietary staple consumed regularly by everyone from nobility to peasant.

Fruits (*Früchte*)

Saxony is a region of fertile farmland, and berries and fruit were and are plentiful. The rich array available in that part of Saxony in the 18th century included cherries, apples, pears, quinces, plums, peaches, strawberries, currants, gooseberries, blackberries, blueberries, rose hips, elderberries, and sloe (a stone fruit). Imported fruits such as figs, dates, pomegranates and lemons were seasonally available.

Almonds (*Mandeln*)

The almond, although it is imported, has long been a part of the cuisine of the German-speaking world, and not only as marzipan, the confection as ubiquitous then as now. Almonds were used in cooking, and almond milk was popular: a mixture of finely pulverized almonds, milk and wine.

Chocolate (*Schokolade, Choccolate*)

Chocolate was still a luxury item and was consumed only as a hot beverage in a tea cup, not as a solid confection. A typical chocolate drink was made with pure cocoa powder or bitter chocolate, plus copious amounts of sugar to make it palatable. The *Frauenzimmer-Lexikon*, a 1715 cookbook, calls it "Choccolate" and suggests that it be "cooked with water, milk or wine."

Sugar (*Zucker*)

Sugarcane plantations in the Far East, Africa and the Americas were meeting the world's increasing demand for molasses and raw sugar. For secure storage and shipment, the plantations liquefied the refined sugar, poured it into rounded conical wooden molds, and allowed it to dry. The resulting "sugar hat" (*Zuckerhut*) was 100% sugar and rock hard.

The sugar hat was stored in the home kitchen in a special wooden sugar box with a hinged knife or a small hatchet, and chunks were broken off and pulverized for use in cooking and beverages. Sugar from beets first became available in the late 1700s, making domestic sugar production possible. (Sugar hats are still sold in Germany today.)

Preserved Foods (*Eingemachtes*)

Because there was no refrigeration, fresh foods had to either be used quickly or preserved. There were four basic methods: drying, smoking, pickling, and salt curing.

The first three methods were widely used. Lean fish and meat were sun-dried, as were peas, beans, lentils, apples, pears, grapes, cherries and plums at harvest-time. Meat, fish, and sausages with a higher fat level were smoked. Vegetables of all kinds were pickled, and sauerkraut and cucumber pickles were common on all tables.

Salt was expensive, and salt curing was practiced mostly by fish merchants, monasteries with a financial incentive, or those who could afford to purchase the large amounts of salt needed for the process. Salt fish (especially herring and cod) were especially prized because they could be transported to landlocked cities like Leipzig during the Lenten fasting season when meat could not be eaten. Fish sausages were also available during Lent.

At the Table (*Tischkultur*)

The cost of living in Leipzig was high and Bach's salary often had to feed many mouths. In 1727, for example, there were at least a dozen people living in the Bach apartment in the St. Thomas School: Bach; Anna Magdalena; 7 children; the sister of Bach's first wife; a cousin; and a nephew. Bach's out-of-town students generally roomed and took their meals there as well. Anna Magdalena would have had a housekeeper/helper who also needed to be fed.

Eating Utensils (*Besteck*)

Until the end of the 1600s, people ate with a metal spoon and a pointed knife. Food was delivered to the mouth in the spoon, on the tip of the knife, or with the fingers.

Forks usually had two or three prongs, a form that reminded people of Satan's fork, so using the utensil for eating was widely forbidden. In the 12th century, Hildegard of Bingen said that using a fork is an insult to God. A 17th-century church father in Austria declared that God had given us ten fingers and we had no need for Satan's tool.

But by the turn of the century the idea was spreading that proper behavior at the table was an indication of one's class and social stature, and greasy hands were coming to be seen as low class and unrefined. A fork enabled one to eat without touching the food with the hands at all, and in the end good table manners turned out to be more important than the fear of Satan. This was a significant moment in the history of eating: the three-piece utensil set had become an established feature of a well laid table. (*ein gut gedeckter Tisch*).

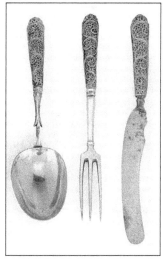

Early 18th-century cutlery set of silver and gold. With the new addition of the fork, a pointed knife is no longer needed to carry food to the mouth.

Pewter (*Zinn, Hartzinn*)

On both sides of the Atlantic in the 1700s, the middle class used durable molded pewter dinnerware (*Geschirr*): plates, platters, bowls, pitchers and drinking vessels. Pewter was the best and cheapest metal for household uses that did not involve extreme heat (pewter is an alloy made mostly from tin, and its melting point is relatively low). Pewterware can also be recycled: a cracked ceramic plate is of no further use, but if a pewter bowl or plate were damaged or worn out it could be sold as scrap to a pewter maker who would melt the metal and reuse it. See page 52 for an inventory of Bach's pewter.

MEALTIMES (*Mahlzeiten*)

The number of daily meals depended on regional customs, socio-economic level, and work schedule. As solid middle-class residents of a large city, the Bach family would have eaten three or sometimes four different types of meals daily.

The menus and meals described below are merely representative examples and do not refer specifically to the Bach family. Beer (full-strength or diluted) was served as a beverage at nearly every meal.

Breakfast (*Frühstück*)

Breakfast was eaten soon after arising in the early morning. It involved as little cooking as possible and was not seen as a "meal" in the sense of a table set with food.

Coffee, tea, or coffee substitutes were often prepared. Bread dipped in raw egg was a quick savory breakfast, and leftovers in the stew or soup pot from the previous day could be reheated—thick soups made from lentils, beans or potatoes (*Brei*) were possible at all meals.

A watery hot cereal was made from scratch by cooking rolled or cracked grains in milk (*Morgensuppe*) or water (*Dunkelsuppe*). A very popular soup eaten at all meals was warm, flat beer thickened with eggs and cream and served with chunks of bread. (See *Biersuppe* recipe on page 51.)

Early Meal (*Frühmahl*)

A late morning meal somewhat like the modern "lunch." Several courses might be served.

Afternoon (*Jause, Brotzeit*)

A snack of cheese, cold meat, bread, and perhaps some wine with bread dipped or broken into it.

Main Meal (*Hauptmahl*)

The main meal of the day was eaten somewhere between 3:00 and 6:00pm. It did not follow the modern custom of serving a series of individual courses from appetizer to dessert. Instead, everything was served at once, with the possible exception of a final dessert course—perhaps a baked good or sweet fruit dish.

I cannot abide drinking tea, coffee, or chocolate. On the other hand,
a beer soup would be wonderful but you cannot get that here because
they don't drink beer in France! A nice plate of sauerkraut and smoked
sausages would be a meal for a king, and I would prefer a cabbage
soup with bacon to all the fancy snacks they serve here in Paris.

– Princess Elizabeth-Charlotte of Bavaria, 1714

CUISINE (*Kochkunst*)

Middle class German families ate a varied diet, especially in a cosmopolitan and prosperous city such as Leipzig. Household cookbooks of the time are filled with colorful, antique vocabulary and spelling but the recipes themselves are not exotic—with a few notable exceptions they would not be out of place on a 21st-century table.

Notable Recipes from German Cookbooks 1715–1739:

Beef, chicken, or vegetable soups of every conceivable kind

Rice soup with saffron and wine

Freshwater crayfish strudel

Fried trout with sauerkraut

Pork with cabbage and carrots

Carp with capers and anchovy sauce (forerunner of Worcestershire sauce)

Carp stuffed with pine nuts and almonds

Trout or freshwater crayfish poached in wine

Veal cutlets with white wine and raisin sauce

Veal sweetbreads with a sauce of onions, saffron, and muscat flowers

For dessert:

Figs simmered in red wine and mixed with almond milk

Stuffed apples, fruit compotes

Fried pastries, simple baked goods

Rice pudding with raisins, and other rice desserts

* See *Further Reading* for information about Princess Elizabeth-Charlotte

RECIPES (*Rezepte*)

The recipes given below are accurate paraphrases of the original German instructions, using modern English vocabulary and grammar. Early cookbooks were often written conversationally, and could be pretty casual about exact quantities. The author and his wife have enjoyed these and other recipes from the early 18th century: the experience was fun and the results delicious.

Milk Soup with Almonds (*Milchsuppe mit Mandeln*)

A common breakfast dish. (Almonds and almond milk were dietary staples.)

- Chop 1/2 cup shelled almonds finely, and simmer in one quart of milk with a bit of sugar. Let cool slightly. Beat two egg yolks with a small amount of butter, and stir the mixture rapidly into the milk until the liquid is foamy. Chop bread into cubes, toss in butter, and toast lightly. Sprinkle over the soup. For a sweeter effect, the bread cubes can be tossed with sugar and caramelized in butter in a hot pan.

Chicken Cooked like a Rabbit (*Ein Hendl, wie man ein Hasen macht*)

Marinades and sauces were used very frequently to provide variety in meat dishes. (The subtitle "cooked like a rabbit" means that the chicken pieces are roasted on a rotating spit over the fire.)

- Prepare a marinade by simmering red wine, water, vinegar and onion. Place skinned chicken breasts and thighs in a bowl, cover with the marinade, and let sit overnight. Remove the chicken from the marinade, place the chicken pieces on a long skewer, and cook over flame. Reduce the marinade, stir in butter and sour cream, add the cooked chicken pieces. Serve on a platter, garnish with lemon slices. The original 1739 recipe concludes with the words,"Ist gut." (It's good.)

Poached Eggs on Croquettes with Mustard Sauce
(*Croquetten mit verlorenen Eier und Senfsosse*)

Croquettes are small rolls or patties made of minced, cooked meat bound with fillers. They are shaped, dipped in bread crumbs and pan or deep fried. The crust is crispy and their name comes from the French word *croquer* (to crunch). A *rissole* is a similar patty wrapped in pastry dough. Both were a popular and versatile way to use leftover cooked meat. Croquettes appear in early 18th-century cookbooks throughout Europe.

Eggs were used mostly as an ingredient in cooking but were sometimes served on their own. Poached eggs were/are properly called *pochierte Eier*, but a traditional nickname for them is *verlorene Eier* (lost eggs). The most popular seasoning for egg dishes was some sort of sauce that included mustard—there were many.

- Make a sauce of onion, fresh parsley, prepared mustard, and white wine, and reduce, add butter. Combine cooked chicken and ham and chop together very fine. Add half as much cooked potato, and a lump of butter. Season. Knead well until it resembles sausage meat. Form into cakes, dip in egg, cover with breadcrumbs, fry until brown and crisp on the outside. Serve croquette on a plate, cover with sauce, place poached egg on top.

Beer Soup (*Biersuppe*)

Beer was plentiful and everyone drank it as a daily beverage, but it lost its carbonation quickly at home in open containers without refrigeration. Beer soup was a very popular way to use up all that flat beer, and it could be eaten at any meal. (See Elizabeth-Charlotte's opinion at the top of page 49.) There are many versions of beer soup, but this is the basic concept:

- Brown 2T flour in 3T butter. Blend in 1 quart flat beer. For a sweet breakfast soup, add a small piece of cinnamon stick and a bit of sugar. Bring mixture to a simmer and stir until a bit thickened. Remove from heat. Whisk together 2 egg yolks and 1/2 cup fresh cream or sour cream. Stir into the hot beer. Commonly eaten with chunks of bread submerged in the soup.

Postscript: The Fear of Want

Ultimately for rich or poor everything depended on the supply of food. In the 17th and 18th centuries, there was a constant awareness that tomorrow could bring some unexpected disaster: a crop failure; a late freeze to kill the fruit crops; a virulent contagious disease; a clash of armies to destroy the food chain and the economy.

Bach's generation remembered their grandparents' tales of the deprivation following the Thirty Years War. Everyone knew that one's dinner plate might be empty tomorrow, and for this reason, celebrations, weddings, and holidays often involved exuberant excesses of eating and drinking.

Bach comically hints at this in his *Peasant Cantata*, (BWV 212), written in 1742 for a large public celebration in a suburb of Leipzig. The soprano and baritone soloists sing these lines:

> *Everybody, let me announce: it's time to start drinking!*
> *If you're thirsty but you can't drink with your right hand,*
> *then just use the other one!*
> *...Let's get ourselves to the tavern,*
> *and let the piping and carousing begin!*

Bach's Metalware

After Bach's death in 1750, the following household items were included in the inventory of his estate.

1 large pewter coffee pot

1 smaller pewter coffee pot

1 brass coffee pot

1 smaller brass coffee pot

1 very small brass coffee pot

1 pewter coffee plate

2 dozen pewter plates

10 pewter bowls of various sizes

4 pewter pitchers

1 pewter wash basin

6 brass candlesticks

4 silver candlesticks

Below: A modern collection of 18th-century pewterware.

Fräulein Liesschen has the last word in
Bach's amusing Coffee Cantata, *BWV 211,*
premiered c.1734 at Zimmermann's coffeehouse:

Kein Freier komm mir in das Haus,

Er hab es mir denn selbst versprochen

Und rück es auch der Ehestiftung ein,

Dass mir erlaubet möge sein,

Den Coffee, wenn ich will, zu kochen.

No suitor shall enter this house
Unless he promises me now,
And puts into the wedding contract,
That I shall be permitted
To brew coffee whenever I like.

Early 18th-century German pewter coffee pot.

Christian Ludwig, Margrave of Brandenburg (1677–1734)

Bach's title page for the set of six concertos he sent to the Margrave

How the "Brandenburgs" Got Their Name

The six compositions known as the "Brandenburg Concertos" are among Bach's most beloved works. The nickname was given to them in the 19th century because of the circumstances of their re-discovery.

Bach was 32 when he arrived in Köthen at the end of 1717 to assume the post of Kapellmeister to His Most Serene Highness, Leopold, Prince of Anhalt-Köthen. He had been working as an organist for the past 14 years, but now his church duties would be light. Religion at the Köthen Court was Calvinist with no artistic trappings. The music in church services was limited to unaccompanied hymns and there was little need for Bach to write liturgical music.

Prince Leopold, on the other hand, loved music, had a strong baritone voice, played the violin, viola da gamba, and keyboard instruments, and sometimes took part in the music-making. Bach led regular in-house Sunday evening concerts in Köthen from 1717 to 1723 for which he wrote a great deal of instrumental music and concertos.

A significant portion of the music Bach wrote in those years has been lost. This was an era of "occasional" music: many such works were written for specific occasions and existed only in unpublished, hand-written form. Once a work had been performed, care was not always taken to save the manuscript. Fortunately, Bach's own impeccably written scores of six of his best concertos from this period did survive, because of special circumstances.

Bach probably met Christian Ludwig, Margrave* of Brandenburg and brother of King Frederick William I of Prussia, in the winter of 1718-19 when Bach was in Berlin to buy a new harpsichord for the Köthen orchestra.

The Margrave heard Bach play, and asked Bach to send him some music. Bach didn't comply until 1721 when his situation in Köthen soured: according to Bach himself, the prince married a woman who disliked music. History generally blames her for Bach's sudden lack of work, but the Prince also was being pressured to send funds to Berlin to support the Prussian military and as a result he had to slash his music budget.

Bach began looking for a new position, and finally responded to the conversation with the Margrave in Berlin. Rather than composing something new, Bach selected six pieces he had already written and performed in Köthen.

In the process of making a new presentation copy for the Margrave, Bach probably revised and reworked the compositions (this would have been a typical procedure for him, he frequently repurposed his own music). The first page of the collection of concertos bears the title:

Six Concerts   *Six Concertos*
Avec plusieurs Instruments   *With several Instruments*

The presentation copy included a letter written in Bach's most courtly French. Dissatisfied with his situation in Köthen, he is reaching out for new possibilities:

To His Royal Highness, My Lord Christian Ludwig,
Margrave of Brandenburg, etc. etc.

Your Royal Highness,

As I had the good fortune a few years ago to be heard by Your Royal Highness, and Your Highness took some pleasure in the meager musical talents which heaven has given me, and as in taking leave of Your Royal Highness, Your Highness deigned to honour me with the command to send Your Highness some pieces of my composition:

I have therefore in accordance with Your Highness's most gracious command taken the liberty of rendering my most humble duty to Your Royal Highness with the present concertos, which I have written for several instruments.

I beg Your Highness most humbly not to judge their imperfection with the rigor of discriminating and sensitive musical taste, which everyone knows Your Highness to have, but rather to take into benign consideration the profound respect and the most humble obedience which I thus attempt to show Your Highness.

Your most obedient servant

Johann Sebastian Bach

The Margrave of Brandenburg, whose musical establishment had neither the quantity nor the quality of the Köthen musicians, apparently never heard these concertos and did not acknowledge Bach's letter. There is no evidence that the scores were ever used, and Bach's manuscripts were not even important enough to be entered into the catalogue of the Margrave's library.

Bach's manuscripts and cover letter were stored in the Brandenburg archives until the package was rediscovered at an open auction in the 19th century. Fortunately, by that time, people were eager to hear concertos by Bach.

The six concertos were nicknamed for the archive in which they had been found, and have been known as the "Brandenburg Concertos" ever since.

* *Margrave* and other German titles of nobility are explained on page 132.

Opposite Page: The first page of the viola part of the *Brandenburg Concerto #3 in G Major,* BWV 1048

Artificial Illumination in the early 18th century

Thin strips of sappy resinous wood

Open-dish oil lamps with wicks of twisted cloth

Candles of rendered animal fat with wicks of twisted cloth

Beeswax candles if one could afford them

Rush stems soaked in animal fat

The light of an open hearth fire

These things did not yet exist:

Any fuel other than animal fats, plant oils, and tree resin

Wax other than beeswax (or bayberry in the New World)

Glass lamp chimneys or braided lantern wicks

Petroleum products such as kerosene

Matches

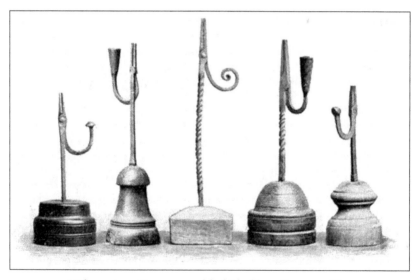

18th-century German rushlight holders. See page 63.

A World Lit Only by Flame

Advancements in artificial illumination in the late 18th century helped propel social and economic changes throughout the world, but in Bach's lifetime all those things had not happened yet.

First of all, there were no "lanterns" in the 19th-century sense with a handle at the top, a lampshade, the round glass chimney around the flame, a controllable flat wick, and an enclosed tank at the bottom for the liquid fuel. Such a device was impossible: in Bach's time there were no glass lamp chimneys, no braided wicks, and no appropriate fuel.

From the dawn of history through most of the 18th century, fuels used for artificial illumination came entirely from the plant and animal world, and most of those fuels were edible. The lighting devices themselves were simple and primitive, had been in use for thousands of years, and involved an exposed and unsteady flame.

This point must be emphasized: living in the immediate presence of an open flame at home was a daily experience for everyone in the 1700s, and it always entailed a certain amount of danger.

Keeping the Flame

There were no matches, and the easiest way to light a flame was from another flame. At home during the daytime, and especially in the winter when the heat came from the open hearth or heating stove, there usually was a flame somewhere in the house from which something else could be lit.

But during the night—when all were in bed—the home was dark: pitch black dark. No open flame could be left burning overnight while people slept; it was simply too dangerous, and in any event no lighting device existed back then that could burn much longer than 20 minutes unattended. So during the nighttime hours there was no open flame in the home except perhaps the glowing, carefully-banked coals of a fire.

In the early morning, if there were no live embers in the fireplace, or in one of the newer ceramic heating ovens, the most common way to generate a flame from scratch was by using flint, steel, and tinder. These things were carefully stored in a metal tinderbox and kept in a safe place but easy to find in the dark.

Sapwood (*Kienholz, Kienspan*)

The modern English translation of *Kienspan* is "kindling," meaning the thinner wood placed under larger logs to help start a fire, but in the 18th century *Kienspan* referred to a small irregular strip of resinous wood meant to burn on its own, one stick at a time, for household illumination. The sticks were thin, usually flat, and uneven in shape and flame. Like all lighting devices of the time, they were relatively dangerous to use.

The most widely used wood was pine, followed by fir, spruce, buckthorn, larch, and cherry. When a tree is injured, resin flows to the damaged area to seal the wound, and in time the resin crystallizes. The resinous areas were removed, and a tool resembling a large woodworker's plane was used to gouge the wood into strips 10 to 12 inches long.

A 12-inch strip of sapwood burns for 15 or 20 minutes, during which time the unsteady, sputtering flame has to be constantly monitored and controlled by changing the horizontal angle of the strip. If both hands were needed, the sapwood could be held between the teeth. For tabletop or hanging use, ceramic holders were made in the shape of a man's head, with the strip inserted into the open mouth. The German slang *maulaffen* (*mouth open*) comes from this artifact, and refers to someone who stands around with his mouth open, doing nothing.

Above: Maulaffen (Kienspan holder).

Left: A hanging oil lamp, called "Crusie" in the New World.

Opposite page: Open dish oil lamp with wicks protruding over the edge.

Fats vary greatly. The value of tallow depends on how old it is and how badly it stinks. It must not come from long-dead animals, nor from animals fed with rotting feed or with cabbages and other strong-tasting things. Further, only kidney and intestinal fat should be used, and not the fat from other parts, which is less suitable. When using fat from the kidneys, it is important to remove all the blood, arteries, nerves, and fibrous web. It should also not be mixed with other flesh or fats.
– from the *Oeconomische Encyclopädie*
(Economic Encyclopedia) by J. G. Krünitz, 1773

The Most Ancient Fuel: Animal Fat and Natural Oils

Oil Lamp (*Öllampe*)

The most primitive and ancient lamp is simply an open vessel containing a burnable oil or fat with some sort of wick protruding out over the edge. Lamps like this have been used for many thousands of years, and terracotta, bronze, stone and alabaster lamps made in ancient Egypt, Greece and Rome were probably the first mass produced objects in history.

Lamps based on this primitive model were still being used in Leipzig and throughout the world in the 18th century.

Various found objects could be used as a wick—a twisted strip of cloth, a plant stem, a bit of rope or twine, even twisted wire—anything that could feed the oily fuel to the flame. (Whenever the word "wick" appears in this book, it refers to a scrap of cloth, not to a manufactured or braided wick.)

An open oil lamp theoretically can burn a wide variety of oils, but the amount of light and odor vary greatly depending on the fuel source. There are only three criteria when choosing fuel for an oil lamp: 1.) it must be relatively fluid at room temperature, 2.) it must be relatively easy to ignite, and 3.) when burning, it must not stink too badly. Basically, any lipid can be used: olive oil, butter, sesame and nut oil, fish oils, or animal fats.

In southern Europe they used oils from olives, sesame, fish and nuts. In Germany and northern Europe, fewer vegetable oils were available—mostly walnut and flax oils—but livestock was plentiful, and the fuel most commonly used for artificial lighting was animal fat.

There were two other devices that illuminated middle-class German homes in the early 1700s. They both burned a form of processed animal fat, but one used the wick to burn the fuel, and the other used the fuel to burn the wick.

...the smoakie light that's fed with stinking tallow.

– Shakespeare, *Cymbeline* (1:6)

Candle (*Kerze*)

Beeswax candles (unfortunately) do not play an important role in 18th-century middle class life. They were rare and expensive, because 1.) the raw material was in limited supply, and 2.) their manufacture was a tedious process. As a result, beeswax candles were used mainly by the church and the upper classes.

Pewter candlesticks

The middle and lower classes had to settle for candles made of animal fat "rendered" by heating it slowly so that it gives up its impurities and moisture and becomes semi-solid at room temperature. In English the resulting substance is called suet or tallow; the German word is *Talg*. This semi-hard fat could be put to use in several ways in the cooler central and northern European climate.

What kind of fat is best: pig, oxen, or sheep? The question is not which fuel smells the best, but which one stinks the least. Pork suet burns with a dark smoke and dim flame. Beef is somewhat better, but mutton suet is by far the best—its smell is the least odious. The best source from any animal was the white fat around the kidneys of healthy livestock that had been raised and slaughtered for food.

Suet candles could be made at home or purchased in bundles from chandlers. The "wick" was merely a narrow twisted strip of cloth, and required almost constant attention and trimming (snuffing) to keep it burning properly. If the candles were not tended they quickly started to burn unevenly and melt. Suet candles were stored in a cool place protected from rodents and other animals eager to eat the tasty animal fat.

Despite these shortcomings, even upper class households resorted to tallow candles for utilitarian needs. They were brighter than open oil lamps and steadier than sapwood strips, but those are low bars to surpass.

Rushlight (*Binsenlicht*)

The rushlight was the poor man's candle. City folk bought them from chandlers, but it was the easiest lighting device to make at home and many country folk made their own.

The rushlight is the opposite of a candle: the fuel is inside the wick. They were made from the stems of the rush plant, a tall marsh plant resembling the bulrush. It has a tough green skin around a white absorbent interior. The stems were harvested, dried, and soaked in warm melted suet. When cooled and solidified, rushlights had to be stored where hungry rats could not get to them. In times of famine, people in rural villages sometimes resorted to gnawing on their rush light stems to keep from starving. Rushlights were still in use in the early 20th century in rural areas of Europe and Britain.

Burning a Rushlight

A 20-inch rush light might burn for 20 minutes, depending on its thickness and the quality of the fat, but like all lighting devices of that time it had to be monitored and tended.

A burning rushlight drips oil; it is fatty and messy, and handling it is a greasy job. If there were children in a family, one of them stayed nearby and every few minutes trimmed or repositioned the rushlight.

The photograph to the right shows a reproduction of an early 18th-century wrought-iron rushlight holder. Tongs grip the rush stem like pliers, and the counterweight doubles as a candlestick. The bottom of the base is a spike that can be inserted into its own base or any other wood surface. Also see the illustration on page 58.

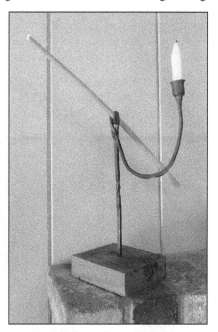

Rushlight and candle holder

Before Bedtime

People carried a candlestick, rushlight or sapwood in their hand when they went to the bedroom, and used the light to help them get into bed. (See page 28.) They could lay a burning rushlight or sapwood on the top of a cabinet or a chest of drawers, with the flaming end extending out as much as needed, and when it burned down to the edge of the furniture it would go out.

The tops of old wooden cabinets often exhibit shallow burned grooves along the edges. These small marks—similar to those from a burning cigarette—are a testament to the feebleness of the flame produced by rushlights and sapwood. Nonetheless, fire was a leading cause of death and an ever-present danger, especially in the bedroom; no flame could be left unattended.

Streetlights (*Strassenbeleuchtung*)

Until the 18th century, European city streets were utterly dark at night, and were the realm of criminals and burglars. No respectable person wished—or dared—to go out after dark.

Between 1660 and 1700, for social and safety reasons (and because the authorities wanted to be aware of activity in the streets), most of northern Europe's major cities began experimenting with regulated streetlight systems. City streetlights helped to conquer the empire of the night and helped fuel the rapid change in society and culture that took place throughout the century.

With perfect timing, coffeehouses began popping up all over Europe in the 1690s, and streetlights allowed them to remain open in the evening. They, in turn became important venues for social, philosophical and political discussion.

An engraving published in 1710 to promote Leipzig streetlights.

Streetlamps were first installed in London in 1662, Paris in 1667, Berlin in 1679, and Vienna in 1687. Paris was illuminated with two thousand streetlamps by 1700.

Leipzig installed 700 streetlamps in 1702, beginning with street intersections and the fronts of major buildings, and hundreds more were installed in the following decades. By 1727, Leipzig was widely known for its street lighting and its elegant, tree-lined and well-lit boulevards.

At that time, the basic streetlamp was a pole or wall bracket supporting a feeble oil lamp enclosed by panes of glass or perforated metal. Each lamp had to be lit, tended, trimmed and refueled, and a brigade of lamplighters kept the tiny flames burning.

The early oil-lamp streetlights produced a flame pitifully weak by our standards, but compared with the total darkness that had preceded them, their light was welcoming, comforting and empowering to individuals and society. It began to give people a sense of control over the dark, and although the brightness was not great, the first streetlights helped society to free the hours of darkness for use by ordinary, law-abiding citizens.

Cresset (*Fackel*)

A "torch" is a primitive lighting device distinguished by its size, portability, and suitability for outdoor use. An archaic English word for torch is *cresset*, and the German word is *Fackel*. In our context it is not the clichéed heavy stick with burning rags on one end.

A cresset is actually a marginally more controllable torch: a metal container of burning oil, grease, wax, or wood, and usually portable. Some cressets stood on three legs, but they were most typically mounted on a pole.

Bach was involved with evening performances outdoors where cressets were used to illuminate the event. The musicians, often playing from hastily written manuscripts, depended on torchlight to see their music.

In October, 1734, Bach's choir and orchestra performed after dark in Leipzig's central market square. The event was lit by 600 cressets held by students, and by large wood-burning cressets on the ground. It was a very eventful evening and is worth describing in more detail later in this book. See page 93.

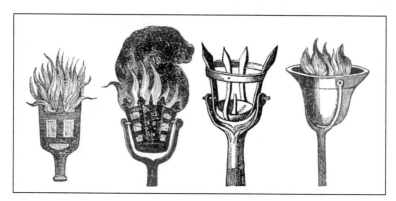

Keyboards Played by Bach

Only two organ consoles exist today on which Bach is known to have played. In both cases the pipes, bellows and other parts of the organ no longer exist. Only the benches, keyboards, front panels, and stops have been preserved.

Left: In the Bach Museum in Arnstadt is the restored organ console from the church where Bach was organist 1703–1707. This instrument was brand new when the 18-year-old Bach began work there.

Below: The Bach Museum in Leipzig displays the organ console from the St. John Church. Bach served as examiner for this organ when it was installed in 1743.

Bach at the Keyboard

During his lifetime, Bach was not primarily known as a composer, at least not of choral or vocal music. He did publish a few very significant keyboard works, but his reputation rested mainly on his prowess at the pipe organ and harpsichord. He was by all accounts an impressive and imaginative virtuoso.

The harpsichord is a subtle and quirky instrument, and it was Bach who put it on the map as a solo vehicle (*Brandenburg Concerto #5* is a good example of this). But the churches of Germany had built their musical experience around organ music since the middle ages. As early as the 13th century, travellers reported hearing "organ songs" in Leipzig churches.

Playing the pipe organ is an aerobic, athletic activity involving hands, arms, upper body, legs and feet. There is swiveling, stretching, arm crossing, independent movement of each hand and foot, and a constant need to maintain one's balance on the bench. No other kind of music making requires this sort of physical activity.

Added to this intensity is the complexity of the music itself: Bach's keyboard works often involve multiple intertwining melodies, each distinctly unique and yet all related, moving back and forth from hand to hand (and foot to foot) as the music is played.

Apparently, no organist could manage all this with the utter ease and elegance exhibited by Bach. His music is so difficult to play today because it is what he played then and he was that good. From his first audition as a teenager in Arnstadt to his mature and notable (and documented) encounters with royalty in Dresden and Berlin, the one thing every witness agreed upon was that Bach was by far the finest keyboardist they had ever seen.

Beyond his musical artistry, Bach had a profound understanding of the design and mechanics of the pipe organ. No two pipe organs are alike, and they are utterly site-specific: the church in which the organ is built is part of the instrument. Depending on the size of the organ, the player is presented with one or more full keyboards for the hands and at least one separate pedalboard for the feet, all of which can be used simultaneously. Bach's mind and ears were easily able to follow five or six interwoven musical lines played simultaneously on the organ's keyboards and foot pedals. For a musical intellect like Bach, the organ and all its potential sounds and colors were a garden of delights.

Sounds are chosen for each of the organ keyboards through the use of labeled knobs called stops. Pulling a stop out several inches allows air to flow to one specific set of organ pipes, known as a register or rank. (If you want really loud music, you can just pull out all the stops.)

Each rank of pipes has its own distinctive range, tone and color. The organist chooses the registration based on the character of the piece, on personal style and taste, and very much on the capabilities of the organ being played.

Because of this, in his few published keyboard works and many manuscripts Bach gives very few suggestions to the player about registration. Then and now, choosing the registers for performances of Bach's great organ works involves a unique combination of repertoire, performer, instrument and place.

EYEWITNESSES

Bach's first biographer, Johann Nikolaus Forkel, wrote in 1802:

> To all this was added the peculiar manner in which he combined the different stops of the organ with each other, or his mode of registration. It was so uncommon that many organ builders and organists were frightened when they saw him pull out the stops. They believed that such a combination of stops could never sound well, but were much surprised when they afterwards perceived that the organ sounded best just so, and had now something peculiar and uncommon, which could never be produced by their own modes of registration.
>
> This peculiar manner of using the stops was a consequence of his minute knowledge of the construction of the organ and of all the single stops. He had early accustomed himself to give to each and every stop a melody suited to its qualities, and this led him to new combinations which, otherwise, would never have occurred to him.

The eminent music critic Johann Adolph Scheibe was not a fan of Bach's compositions, but in his 1737 publication *Critischer Musicus* he expressed his admiration for Bach's technique at the keyboard:

> He is an extraordinary artist on the harpsichord and on the organ... I have heard this great man play on various occasions. One is amazed at his ability and one can hardly conceive how it is possible for him to achieve such agility, with his fingers and with his feet, in the crossings, extensions, and extreme jumps that he manages, without mixing in a single wrong tone, or displacing his body by any violent movement.

"THE MIRACLE OF LEIPZIG..."

This physical poise mentioned by Scheibe is a sign of a sophisticated technique, not only of the hands but also the feet. In 1732, Bach travelled to the city of Kassel to test a rebuilt organ. A decade later, Constantin Bellerman recalled Bach's use of the organ pedals:

> Bach deserves to be called the miracle of Leipzig as far as music is concerned. For, if he likes, he can use his feet alone (while his fingers do either nothing or something else) to achieve such an admirable, lively, and

rapid harmony of sounds on the organ that others would seem unable to imitate it even with their fingers. He flew over the pedals as if his feet had wings, making the organ resound with a fullness of sound that penetrated the ears of all present like a thunderbolt. Prince Frederick of Kassel admired him with such amazement that he took a precious ring from his finger and gave it to Bach as soon as the music was over. If Bach earned such a gift merely for the agility of his feet, what, I ask, would the Prince have given him if he had brought his hands into service as well?

Bach's keyboard music requires an agile fingering technique. He was not the first keyboardist to use his thumbs as much as the other eight fingers, but the practice was not universal and he did much to encourage it. It was not an abstract or theoretical issue for him: his complex music with its multiple intertwining lines simply requires frequent crossing of the thumb and fingers.

Bach's son Carl Philipp Emanuel remembered:

My late father told me about having heard great men in his youth who did not use the thumb except when it was necessary for large stretches. Since he lived at a time in which there gradually took place a quite remarkable change in musical taste, he was obliged to think out a much more complete use of the fingers, and especially to use the thumb (which apart from other uses is quite indispensable especially in the difficult keys) in such a manner as Nature, as it were, wishes to see it used. Thus it was raised suddenly from its former idleness to the position of the principal finger.

Many years after his death, pupils of Bach—and their pupils—quoted aphorisms from Bach himself. The best-known today are:

I was obliged to work and study industriously. With enough hard work any halfway talented person can do what I do.

and,

After all, it's easy to play a keyboard. There's nothing remarkable about it: all you have to do is touch the right key at the right time and the instrument will play itself.

Detail from *Wer nur den lieben Gott lässt walten*, BWV 642, from *Das Orgel-Büchlein (The Little Organ Book)* written for the very young Wilhelm Friedeman. There are three separate melodies: the hands play the top and middle lines, and the feet the bottom.

STARTLING VARIATIONS

Old myths sometimes cloud our view of Bach's place in music history. For example, legend has it that Bach's young and trendy composer sons thought he was just "an old white wig" writing outdated music. That is not true.

In fact his sons respected and adored him. Further, he could be forward thinking and experimental, and actually received criticism about it on more than one occasion. The first notable incident occurred when he was only 20.

In October, 1705, Bach was in his third year as organist at the St. Boniface Church in the little town of Arnstadt. The eager young Bach was at the beginning of his career, and wanted to meet and study with the great composer/organist Dietrich Buxtehude in Lübeck (about 200 miles to the north). The Arnstadt City Council granted Bach a leave of absence for four weeks to travel to Lübeck, but Bach remained in Lübeck for *four months*, and when he finally returned to Arnstadt he was filled with new ideas about harmony and ornamentation, especially in the hymns. The following lines are taken from the minutes of the Arnstadt Town Council meeting on Feb 21, 1706.

> *The organist Bach traveled to the city of Lübeck in order to comprehend one thing or another about his art. He had been given leave to stay away for four weeks, and in fact stayed four times too long. And upon his return... complaints have been made to the council that Mr. Bach now accompanies the hymns with startling variations and irrelevant ornaments which obliterate the melody and confuse the congregation. We do reprove Mr. Bach for having added these many curious variations, and for having mingled many new sounds into the music.*

> *We furthermore do ask Herr Bach by what right he recently caused an unfamiliar young woman to be invited into the choir loft and let her make music there.*

Who was she? Traditional lore has long maintained that the "young woman" was Maria Barbara Bach, a cousin of J.S. Bach whom he married two years later. However, the document from the Council refers to the female in question as "an unfamiliar young woman" (*ein fremdes Mädchen*), and Maria Barbara had been living in Arnstadt for years and was not "unfamiliar" there at all. Further, there is no record that Maria Barbara was musical, and no indication that she participated in Bach's professional life in the way his second wife did.

The true identity of the "unfamiliar young woman" in the choir loft with Bach will always be a mystery, although Christoph Wolff and other scholars assume Bach was working legitimately with a female vocalist. In some churches at that time (but not in Leipzig), women were allowed to assist in the music, as "adjuncts."

Dueling Keyboards

Jean Baptiste Volumier (born in Denmark as Johann Wollmyer) was Kapellmeister to the Dresden court of Frederick Augustus I of Saxony. French music was all the rage in Dresden, and Volumier, who had studied in Paris, was the ideal man to bring more of the fashionable French music to the court.

But in 1717, Volumier's comfortable Dresden existence was upended when the renowned Parisian harpsichordist Louis Marchand visited Dresden and performed for Prince Augustus, who was so impressed that he offered Marchand a lucrative position in the court ensemble. Volumier felt threatened by Marchand's encroachment on his turf, and sent an invitation to his colleague Johann Sebastian Bach, the organist of the Weimar Court. Bach accepted—he was in search of new employment and eager to show off his skills to the Dresden elite, and Volumier's plan gave him a chance to do just that.

When Bach arrived in Dresden, he and Volumier secretly attended an organ concert by Marchand. Following the performance, at Volumier's encouragement, Bach wrote a letter inviting Marchand to a keyboard "duel." Bach proposed that each man would give to the other a series of musical challenges, such as melodies to improvise upon, and various styles to emulate. Marchand accepted, and the palace of the senior minister, General von Flemming, was chosen as the venue.

News of the contest reached Prince Augustus's ears. He agreed to attend, and also offered a considerable cash prize to the winner.

On the day of the contest, in the presence of the Royal Family and the Dresden aristocracy, Bach arrived at the appointed time but his opponent did not. Apparently Marchand had realized that he was outclassed by Bach's superior skill—he left Dresden by stagecoach at dawn and was on his way back to Paris. The Dresden nobility who had gathered in General von Flemming's palace enjoyed a solo recital by Kapellmeister Bach.

Volumier had successfully rid himself of Marchand, but Bach had nothing to show for all his effort. He received no commissions or appointments in Dresden, and the promised prize money was stolen by one of General von Flemming's palace courtiers.

According to his son Carl Philipp Emanuel, in later years Bach was too modest to brag about the strange event; Emanuel recalled that his father "told the story but seldom, and then only when urged."

St. Thomas square, with St. Thomas School in the
background and the church on the right, 1732

Fashionable St. Catherine Street, 1727. The third and fourth doors from
the left are the entrance to Zimmermann's coffeehouse. (See page 88)

Leipzig Market Place, 1712. See page 94.

THE INTIMATION OF CLEANLINESS

MATTER OUT OF PLACE

It is no exaggeration to say that the 17th and early 18th centuries mark the low point of personal hygiene in the history of the Western world.

An old saying among social historians is "Dirt is merely matter out of place." Humans certainly have a desire to preserve order in their environment, to eliminate "out of place" dirt and trash, but in Bach's time, the idea of cleanliness had nothing to do with our modern notions of health or disease prevention. 18th-century theories of disease were based on 2000-year-old fantasies about how the body works, and had little to do with reality. (See: *Medicine and Mortality* p. 103)

Cleanliness in the 18th century was a matter of appearance, not health. People tried hard to look clean, but in fact they almost never were. The means of achieving an aesthetically pleasing level of personal cleanliness were just not yet in place. Not only was there a lack of running water, but most people actually believed bathing was unhealthy. More about that in a moment.

As a result, everybody basically stank all the time, but they took valiant steps to hide the smell from each other and from themselves. Those steps rarely included washing any part of their bodies with water.

Cities and towns stank as well. Attempts were being made in European cities to manage and improve the disposal of urban sewage and household waste, but open channels still ran through the streets and market squares of many cities in Europe. Travellers in the early 1700s said they could smell Paris long before they could see it.

Illustrations of Leipzig during Bach's time clearly show narrow open channels in the cobblestone streets. Chamber pots and other waste matter were dumped into these gutters, and rain helped to flush them and keep the city clean.

On the opposite page:
Open gutters are shown in the square by the St. Thomas Church; in front of Zimmermann's coffeehouse; and running through Leipzig's market square and past the house where the Prince of Saxony stayed when Bach's musicians serenaded him. Illustrations of that time show small flat footbridges across the narrow gutters here and there. By mid-century, Leipzig had routed most of these channels underground.

The image on the cover of this book, made c.1710, shows no realistic details of the pavement. Gabriel Bodenehr used artistic license to create a clean (and odor-free) street surface for his tiny citizens to preen and promenade. The realistic depictions of this plaza by other artists in those decades clearly show the gutters.

To Be Clean (*Sauber sein*)

It's important to understand that the aesthetic concept of "cleanliness" in the 17th and early 18th centuries in Europe had very little to do with water.

A letter written by Princess Elisabeth-Charlotte of Bavaria in August, 1705, gives us an example. The Princess had traveled all day on dusty roads in the hot sun and she arrived at her destination exhausted and dirty. In fact, her face was so dirty that she actually had to wash it with water, an occurrence so unusual that she felt the need to mention it in her letter.

I was forced to wash my face, it was so dusty, like a grey mask.

Were it not for the dust, no water would have been necessary. Normally, after a day of travel, a woman of fashion would have removed her dress, her long white linen chemise, and any other underclothing (which varied by region and country). She or her attendant would have wiped her body vigorously with a dry, perfumed cloth. She then would have put on a fresh white chemise or undergarment, and then a clean dress over that.

Faces and hands were kept clean, sometimes with a bit of water. But the skin on the rest of the body went for long periods—sometimes months or more—without being touched by water at all. Europeans had forgotten about the benefits of water, and as a result they created a personal and social environment that would be unthinkable to modern people.

It was not always this way.

Two thousand years ago the Romans had it all figured out: they liked to be clean, and they provided forms of running water in their homes to bring drinking water in and flush garbage and human waste out. The Romans also built communal baths in their major outposts, and even after the collapse of the Roman empire the use of the baths continued into the middle ages.

Then the Black Death appeared in the 1300s and wiped out half the population of Europe in a few years. In a world with no knowledge of germs, the plague was terrifying and caused wide paranoia and panic. The communal baths became suspect and the theory spread that the *water itself* might enable the transmission of diseases.

This opinion evolved, and by 1600 the general European understanding of cleanliness and health was this: that baths promote disease because the warm water cleanses and opens the pores of the skin, allowing the miasma of a sick person to be absorbed through the open pores. People believed that dirt on the skin actually served as a barrier to these threats.

In much of Europe, people essentially stopped bathing with water and began using other techniques:

1.) rubbing the skin vigorously with a dry, perfumed cloth

2.) applying more perfume

3.) putting on a clean undershirt

4.) wiping the skin occasionally with a slightly damp cloth, particularly in an extreme case such as the princess describes above

Perfume and floral aromatics were used extensively, and men and women carried perfume bottles and dried flower sachets in their pockets. Perforated porcelain vases were filled with dried flowers and herbs and placed in every room. Cinnamon water was a particularly popular concoction, used as a mouthwash or sprinkled on little pillows which were kept in one's armpits.

The myth of the dangers of bathing in water would begin to fade in Bach's time led by the customs of the upper class and the advances of the Age of Enlightenment. By the second half of the century, sponge baths were recommended, and the theory of water as peril faded from common knowledge.

BATHING (*Baden*)

It was no small task to bathe at home in a tub of warm water in the 1720s, and the following is a very general description of what it might have entailed.

There was no such thing as a "bathtub" or a "bathroom." The vessel was most likely a wooden tub or a large copper basin, and sometimes the laundry tub was used.

Whatever the container, it must be filled with water. A modern bathtub holds 40–50 gallons. In order to get 40 gallons of water to bathing warmth (80–90°F.) you will need at least 10 or 15 gallons of boiling water.

For this, cold water has to be carried in buckets from a public fountain, communal hand pump, or well. A gallon weighs about 8 pounds, so this project involves carrying a minimum of 320 pounds of water bucket by bucket from the pump or fountain to one or more kettles heating over a fire. As each kettle comes to a boil, it is carried to the tub and poured in. Then the kettle is refilled with cold water and heated again. Of course while the next batch of water is heating, the first batch is already cooling in the tub.

It's clear why more people did not bathe more often at home. The entire process involved time, expense and a lot of effort, from chopping the wood to disposing of the dirty water. In a way, it was easier and less stressful to remain dirty and "wash" in the usual haphazard and ineffectual manner with dry cloths and an occasional dab of water here and there.

If you have a loose tooth, do not put opium on it or rub it with anything. Instead, rinse your mouth often with wine, and keep a few drops in the mouth. This will strengthen your gums.

– Elizabeth-Charlotte of Bavaria, 1714

DENTAL CARE (*Zahnpflege*)

In the 18th century, everyone had bad breath and spent their lives dealing unsuccessfully with the symptoms and the causes. Decay and toothaches were thought to be caused by the Tooth Worm (*Zahnwurm*), a creature that lived inside human teeth and caused all sorts of trouble about which there was very little to be done.

Toothbrush (*Zahnbürste*)

The toothbrush shaped as we know it is a 20th century thing. Europeans in the 1700s often made a "brush" by chewing or shredding one end of a thin willow twig to soften it. With a knife, the end of the twig could be sliced finely into a more brush-like tool, and the other end sharpened to make a toothpick.

Toothpick (*Zahnstocher*)

The toothpick is an ancient and valuable tool, and was so ubiquitous in the 18th century that it became a piece of adornment in high society. Artisans and jewelers made toothpicks of ivory, silver or copper, to be carried in a pocket or worn on a thin chain around the neck.

Tooth Powder (*Zahnputzmittel*)

Powders and pastes made with a combination of abrasives, coloring and flavor have been used throughout history, with wildly different ingredients based on nationality and era. In 18th-century Europe, people cleaned their teeth with a powdered mixture of substances such as marble, pumice, brick, magnesium carbonate, chicken and wren eggshells, oyster shells, and charcoal. Flavorings included peppermint oil, menthol, honey, sugar, or gentian oil. The powder was often mixed by the apothecary and dispensed in a small paper cone or box, and was applied by massaging the teeth and gums with the fingers or a sponge or cloth.

Dentist (*Zahnartzt*)

In the early 1700s there were no trained "dentists" in any medical sense. Dentists were mostly itinerant toothpullers with little education beyond a few months of apprenticeship. They were a lethal combination of barber-surgeon, blacksmith and con man, and they were considered to be of low degree in society. The words charlatan, quack, mountebank and quack-salver were originally coined as pejorative nicknames for these European toothpullers.

The first order of business for proper dental work was to tie the patient to a chair. For certain procedures, a "medical assistant" was engaged whose only qualification was that he was strong enough to hold the patient's head in a tight grip. There was no hand-washing, no instrument sterilization—nobody thought of such things, or knew about germs or where infections come from. There was no anesthetic, other than a huge amount of wine or brandy. In the worst cases, nightshade, hashish, or opium were administered.

Then the practitioner approached the patient's mouth with a frightening array of pliers, tweezers, and pincers. If some resembled a farrier's hoofing tools, they probably were.

Complications from "dental work" in the 1700s included injured or dislocated jaw; concussion from violent movement of the head; and eye injuries. Patients commonly experienced fever, local and systemic infection, abscesses, chronic bleeding, and occasionally death. It's no wonder that people tried every folk remedy possible to avoid actually being treated by a "dentist."

For routine tooth pain and inflammation, sage oil, clove oil, myrtle and cinnamon were used. People with bad breath from their rotting teeth washed their mouths with bramble leaf honey mixed with wood ash—which ultimately rotted the teeth even more but temporarily gave them sweet breath.

Dental Postscript

In a poetic reversal of fortune, in the 18th century it was the upper classes whose teeth rotted first. While the common people chewed on dark whole-grain breads, potatoes, and apples, and washed it down with diluted beer, the wealthy were eating sweets and drinking coffee and chocolate with lots of sugar.

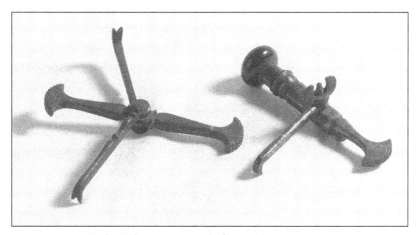

Early 18th-century tools for tooth extractions.

The east end of the St. Thomas Church today.
Compare with the engravings on the front cover and page 9.

...the authorities are odd, and not much interested in music.
– Bach in a letter to a friend in 1730,
describing the Leipzig City Council

Bach Looks Elsewhere

The Letter to Georg Erdman

In 1730, dissatisfied and disappointed with his relationship with the Leipzig City Council, Bach wrote a long and heartfelt letter to an old school friend, Georg Erdmann, in the hope of finding new employment. This is the only document written by Bach in which he unburdens himself in detail on a personal level.

In 1695, the newly-orphaned Bach had been uprooted from home and sent to live with his older brother in Ohrdruf. Bach and Erdman met in school there, and the two ten-year-olds became close friends. In 1700 the two boys, now teenagers, set out on foot on the long trek (around 200 miles) to Lüneburg where they both enrolled in school. Bach left Lüneburg in 1702, and the two had not seen each other since c.1716.

Job-seeking motivated this letter, and Bach lists several complaints about his situation: the city fathers have no interest in music, Leipzig is an expensive place to live, his contract is not as lucrative as was originally promised, and he had not received certain fees due to him. The last two are serious charges. Bach the businessman had not done his due diligence, and now he seems to be paving the way for justifying his release from the contract.

It is not known if Erdmann replied. In any event, Bach served the City Council of Leipzig for the rest of his life.

Leipzig, October 28, 1730

Most Honorable Friend,

You will have the kindness to forgive an old and faithful servant for taking the liberty of troubling you with the present letter. It is nearly four years since you favored me with a kind answer to the letter I sent you; I remember that at that time you graciously asked me to give you some news of what had happened to me, and I humbly take this opportunity of providing you with the same.

You know the course of my life from my youth until the change in my fortunes that took me to Köthen as Kapellmeister. There I had a gracious Prince, who both loved and understood music, and in his service I intended to spend the rest of my life.

It must happen, however, that the said Serenissimus should marry a Princess of Berenburg, and that then the impression should arise that the musical interests of the said Prince had become somewhat lukewarm, especially as the new Princess seemed to be unmusical ("eine Amusa"); and it pleased God that I should be called hither to be Director Musices and Cantor at the St. Thomas School.

At first, it did not seem at all proper for me to exchange my position of Kapellmeister for that of Kantor. But this post was described to me in such favorable terms that finally (particularly since my sons seemed inclined to [university] studies) I cast my lot in the name of the Lord, and made the journey to Leipzig, took my examination, and then made the change of position.

Here, by God's will, I am still in service. But since

(1) I find that the post is by no means so lucrative as it had been described to me;

(2) I have failed to obtain many of the fees pertaining to the office;

(3) the place is very expensive;

and (4) the authorities are odd, and not much interested in music, so that I must live amid almost constant vexation, envy, and persecution; accordingly I shall be forced, with God's help, to seek my fortune elsewhere.

Should Your Honor know or find a suitable post in your city for an old and faithful servant, I beg you most humbly to put in a most gracious word of recommendation for me--I shall not fail to do my best to give satisfaction and justify your most gracious intercession in my behalf.

My present income totals about 700 thaler, and when there are somewhat more funerals than usual, the fees rise in proportion; but when a healthy wind blows, they decrease accordingly, as for example last year, when I lost fees that would ordinarily come in from funerals to an amount of more than 100 thaler. In Thuringia [the region of his birth] I could get along better on 400 thaler than here with twice that many, because of the excessively high cost of living.

Now I must add a little about my domestic situation. I am married for the second time, my late wife having died in Köthen. From the first marriage I have three sons and one daughter living, whom Your Honor will graciously remember having seen in Weimar. From the second marriage I have one son and two daughters living.

My eldest son is a law student, and of the other two [from the first marriage], one is in the senior class and the other in the junior, and the eldest daughter is still unmarried. The children of my second marriage are still small, the eldest, a boy, being six years old. But they are all born musicians, and I can assure you that I can already form both vocal and instrumental ensembles within my family, particularly since my present wife sings a good clear soprano, and my eldest daughter, too, joins in not badly.

I shall almost transgress the bounds of courtesy if I burden Your Honor any further, and I therefore hasten to close, remaining with most devoted respect my whole life long

Your Honor's most obedient and devoted servant

Joh. Seb. Bach

The Puzzle Monogram

This monogram was designed and drawn by J. S. Bach himself in the 1730s, when he was hoping to receive a title or appointment at the Court of the Elector of Saxony in Dresden. Beneath a royal crown, Bach created a three-letter monogram "JSB" and then superimposed upon it the mirror image of those letters.

The B Minor Mass Cover Letter

When Bach left his job as Kapellmeister of the Köthen Court and began work in Leipzig, he took a step down in prestige. Instead of making music with Prince Leopold and his fine professional musicians, he was fighting petty battles with a City Council that expected him to teach Latin to schoolboys and be on duty to inspect their dormitories. He longed for respectability in the eyes of the city fathers, and some sort of royal appointment or title would give him a boost in Leipzig even if it didn't actually offer a new job somewhere else.

Bach was 48 and had been toiling in Leipzig for ten years when a major event in February 1733 touched all of Saxony: in the princely palace in Dresden, Kurfürst Frederick Augustus died after a long and respectable life. Known as "Augustus the Strong," he was the Elector of Saxony, the highest ruler in the province. He was also a renowned patron of the arts and under his reign Dresden had become a noble and cultured city. (The titles of the Electors are among the most complicated in German nobility and are difficult to translate into English. See the Appendix for an explanation.)

Frederick Augustus I was automatically succeeded by his only legitimate son, the 37 year old Frederick Augustus II.

On July 27, 1733, with the help of friends and patrons in Dresden, Bach arranged to send a package of music to his new sovereign. He and Anna Magdalena delivered the manuscript to Dresden themselves, and they completed some of the pages in Dresden at the last minute. The cover letter, written and signed by Bach, is one of his greatest masterpieces of obsequious humility.

To His Most Serene Highness, the Prince and Lord, Frederick Augustus, Royal Prince in Poland and Lithuania, Duke in Saxony, etc etc...

My Most Gracious Lord, Most Serene Elector, Most Gracious Lord!

To Your Royal Highness I submit in most profound devotion the present small work of that science which I have achieved in musique, with the most entirely submissive prayer that Your Highness will look upon it with most gracious eyes, according to Your Highness's world-famous clemency and not according to the meager composition; and thus deign to take me under Your most mighty protection.

For some years and up to the present time, I have had the Directorium of the music in the two principal churches in Leipzig, but have innocently had to suffer one injury or another, and on occasion also a diminution of the fees payable to me in this office; but these injuries would disappear completely if Your Royal Highness would grant me the favor of conferring upon me a title of Your Highness's Court Kapelle, and would allow Your High command for the issuing of such a document go forth to the proper place.

Such a most gracious fulfillment of my most humble prayer will bind me to unending devotion, and I offer myself in most indebted obedience to show at all times upon Your Royal Highness's most gracious desire my untiring zeal in the composition of music for the church as well as for the orchestra, and to devote my entire forces to the service of Your Highness,

Remaining in unceasing fidelity,

Your Royal Highness's most humble and obedient servant

Johann Sebastian Bach

Dresden, July 27, 1733

The "trifling product" that Bach enclosed was the set of beautifully prepared musical scores for a Kyrie and Gloria—the first two sections of what future generations would call the *Mass in B Minor.*

But although the Dresden Court eventually (in 1736) issued a certificate appointing him "Composer to the Royal Court Capelle... with his Royal Majesty's Most August Signature," all Bach really got from the whole affair was the certificate, an honorary title, and a small stipend.

Leipzig is where Bach remained until his death in 1750.

Humble and Obedient... (*unterthänigst-gehorsamster*)

There are other letters from Bach to the rulers of Saxony, signed simply "your most humble and obedient J. S. Bach."

He often signed other letters to friends and colleagues as "your most humble and obedient servant J. S. Bach," using the German word *Diener* (*servant*) in an old-fashioned and respectful sense.

However, Bach signs this letter to the Prince with the word *Knecht*, translated above as *servant*. But *Knecht* actually connotes something much lower than servant—more like the filthy, dim-witted, churlish farm hand who slept in the barn with the animals. A *Knecht* is assumed to have no dignity or free will, and the word could reasonably be translated as *slave*. This was the relationship between subject and sovereign.

On both sides of the Atlantic, a political movement was growing that would transform serfs into free men and subjects into citizens, but very little of that was happening in Bach's world yet.

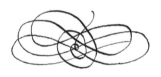

Ei, wie schmeckt der Coffee süsse,
Lieblicher als tausend Küsse,
Milder als Muskatenwein.
Coffee, Coffee muss ich haben,
Und wenn jemand will mich laben,
Ach so schenkt mir Coffee ein.

Ah, how sweet the coffee tastes,
Lovelier than a thousand kisses,
Smoother than Muscatel wine.
Coffee, coffee, I have to have it,
And if anyone wants to make me happy,
Just serve me some coffee!

From Bach's *Coffee Cantata*, BWV 211,
premiered c.1734 at Zimmermann's coffeehouse,
for an audience of drinking, smoking, and card-
playing music lovers. "Coffee" is an archaic
German spelling used in the original text.

Pleasures (*Genüsse*)

The Coffee Saxons (*die Kaffee-Sachsen*)

When the Ottoman siege of Vienna failed in 1683, the fleeing Turkish army left behind sacks of dark dry beans. An enterprising Austrian army officer recognized the beans and opened central Europe's first coffeehouse. In just over a decade coffee made its first appearance in Leipzig.

Leipzig and coffee are inseparable, and the city claims one of the oldest coffeehouses in Germany. The Arabian Coffee Tree (*Zum arabischen Coffe Baum* [sic]) first served coffee in 1694. The following year, Gottfried Zimmermann opened Leipzig's second coffeehouse. By the 1720s, eight coffeehouses were playing an important role in Leipzig's cultural life.

Coffee became so popular in Saxony that in the 1750s Saxon mercenaries told King Frederick the Great of Prussia that they could not go into battle for him without being provided with coffee: *Ohne Gaffee gönn mer nich gämpfn!* they complained (*Without coffee we can't fight!*). The king derisively called them *Kaffee-Sachsen* and the nickname stuck.

Coffee was traditionally served sweet in Leipzig. S*iesse muss d'r Coffe sein*, says an old Saxon proverb. (*Coffee must be sweet.*) If coffee didn't measure up to their standards, it was derided as *flower coffee* (*Blümchenkaffee*)—coffee so thin that one could see through it to the image of the little flowers at the bottom of Meissen porcelain cups. An anecdote tells of an economical host who roasted and ground fourteen beans for fifteen cups of coffee.

Coffeehouses and cafés were influential in the development of social and intellectual thought throughout the 18th century. Until this point in history, social gatherings inevitably involved or revolved around alcoholic beverages, and these new meeting places continued to serve alcohol, but coffee was the main drink and the reason for being there. Leipzig was a cosmopolitan city with the second oldest university in Germany, and its coffeehouses were frequented by a mix of intellectuals, artists, merchants, businessmen, bankers, scholars and visitors (all men of course, no women were admitted except for concerts). As the Age of Enlightenment was dawning, the thousands of coffeehouses throughout Europe served as venues for political and artistic discussion, activities and ideas.

By the 1720s, Zimmermann's coffeehouse was the largest and best-appointed in Leipzig, and it provides us with a good example of a large coffeehouse in a major city. It occupied the first two stories of a five-story building on Leipzig's fashionable St. Catherine Street, one block from the main market square.

A coffeehouse like Zimmermann's was nothing like the 21st century version. The rooms were large, crowded, noisy, smelly, smoky and sometimes lively. Patrons could enjoy coffee, tea, hot chocolate, wine, beer, and other alcoholic drinks, and a wide variety of food was available.

Bach's Collegium Musicum

A Collegium Musicum is an ensemble of certain musically knowledge-able persons, who, according to their particular training in vocal or in instrumental music, come together at a particular time and place and under the supervision of a particular director in order to perform musical works. One encounters collegia of this sort in many places. Of all those in Leipzig, the Bach Collegium Musicum is the most renowned.

From the *Grossesvollständiges Universal Lexicon*, by Johann Heinrich Zedler, Leipzig 1739. *(The Large Complete Universal Encyclopedia)*

In addition to various smaller eating and drinking rooms on the second floor, Zimmermann's had a public area on the ground floor that was large enough for as many as 40 or 50 performers and an audience of 150. This was the winter performing venue of Leipzig's Collegium Musicum.

The Collegium Musicum was an independent ensemble of the finest university musicians and local professionals. Georg Philipp Teleman founded the group in 1702 when he was a student at Leipzig University.

Bach was guest conductor of the Collegium during his early years in Leipzig, and from 1729 to 1741 he was the director of the group (today he would be credited as composer, arranger and bandleader). This was a private contract unconnected to his work for the city.

In the winter months they performed in the coffeehouse on Friday evenings from 8:00 to 10:00. In the warmer months they held early-evening concerts on Wednesdays at Zimmernann's open-air coffee garden outside the city walls. During Leipzig's three big trade fairs in winter, spring and fall, concerts were given more often.

The Collegium Musicum offered a broad and up-to-date variety of music by Bach and his sons, by the composers of the orchestra in Dresden, and by other contemporary European composers. Repertoire included secular cantatas (such as Bach's *Coffee Cantata, BWV 211*), chamber music, works for solo instruments, orchestral suites, concertos for violin, harpsichord, oboe, etc., all for an audience who drank coffee, wine or beer, enjoyed food, and generally socialized.

Listeners were permitted (and even encouraged) to smoke tobacco and play cards during the music, as it was seen to boost the atmosphere of fun. Although women were not permitted to enter coffeehouses during regular hours, they were allowed to attend Bach's Collegium concerts, and women vocalists sometimes took part in the performances.

The concerts at Zimmermann's were serious events, and not merely background music to the regular café operations. The performances of the Collegium were, in fact, a prototype of our modern concept of a concert.

Bach scholars believe that during the 1730s the Collegium Musicum and the music it performed became the central focus of Bach's life. In 1741, Zimmermann died, Bach's health was beginning to fade, and he relinquished his Collegium duties that year. In the final decade of his life, Bach's artistic activity became more instrumental and solitary.

An Ottoman and a cherub share coffee in this famous detail over the main entrance to The Arabian Coffee Bean *(Zum arabischen Coffe Baum)*[sic]. In continuous operation since 1694, it was Leipzig's first coffeehouse and is one of the oldest in Germany.

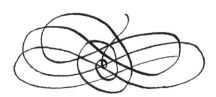

Zimmermann's coffeehouse occupied the first two floors of the center building. The two doors with similar awnings are the main entrance.

During the early 1700s, one-third of all Leipzig's inner-city buildings were remodeled or rebuilt. The streets were paved and there was public lighting at the street intersections and on important buildings. Amsterdam publisher Peter Schenk produced a book of Leipzig scenes in 1712 featuring this engraving by Johann Georg Schreiber. Despite the modernizations, it would be several decades before the open storm drain channels were re-directed underground.

BACH AND THE CASK OF WINE
"This noble gift of God"

In his career as an employed composer and church musician, Bach created his vocal music mainly for worship (church) or adoration (royalty), and he rarely had an opportunity to express his sense of humor. We glimpse a bit of it only in the few works he wrote for pure entertainment, such as the *Coffee Cantata* (written for Zimmermann's Coffeehouse) and the *Peasant Cantata* (for a civic celebration in a Leipzig suburb).

Bach and his cousin (and former assistant) Johann Elias Bach shared a love of good drink. After many years of friendship, Bach wrote a wry thank-you note to Johann Elias, from which the following paragraphs are excerpted. (Letter-writers often used French as a language of respect. "Schweinfourth" is the town of Schweinfurt, 200 miles southwest of Leipzig.)

November 1, 1748
Monsieur Johann Elias Bach
Chanteur et Inspecteur des Gymnasiastes
de la Ville Impérialle a Schweinfourth
Franque Coburg

My dear and most esteemed cousin
[...]

Thank you for sending me the excellent cask of wine, for which I send you many thanks.

It is however, greatly to be regretted that the little cask was somehow damaged during shipment, either by being jostled in the wagon or in some other way, for when it was opened for the usual customs inspection here it was found to be almost two-thirds empty—according to the inspector's report it contained not more than six quarts. It is a pity that even one drop of this noble gift of God should have been wasted.

I send my best regards to you and remain, with best greetings to you from us all, your most faithful cousin,

Johann Sebastian Bach

PS:

Although you kindly offered to send me more of this delicious wine, I think I really must decline your gracious offer on account of the excessive expenses here. You see, the shipping charges were 16 groschen, the delivery man charged 2 groschen, the customs inspector 2 groschen 3 pfennig, the inland duty 5 groschen 3 pfennig, and the general excise tax 3 groschen.

My honored cousin can judge for himself that the those six quarts cost me almost 5 groschen each, which for a gift is really much too expensive.

Tobacco

Explorers returning from the New World in the 1500s introduced tobacco to Europe. It was first used as snuff but by 1600 it was being smoked in England and northern Europe. The earliest forms of the rolled cigarette appeared in Spain in the 1600s, although most smokers used the ubiquitous long, thin-stemmed clay pipe (as described in the adjacent poem). Engravings of the time show women smoking pipes, but it was not considered a proper activity for middle-class ladies.

The first tobacco factory in northern Germany was established in 1720 by King Frederick William I (the father of Frederick the Great), who was famous for enjoying his pipe.

On the opposite page is the text of a song that appears in the notebook of music compiled in 1725 by Anna Magdalena and her husband.

It is titled *Erbauliche Gedanken eines Tobackrauchers (Edifying Thoughts of a Tobacco Smoker)*. The tune is generally thought to be by Bach or one of his sons. In the original notebook, the melody is written in Anna Magdalena's hand and the harmony has been filled in by Bach. The authorship of the text is unknown, but some speculate that it is by Bach.

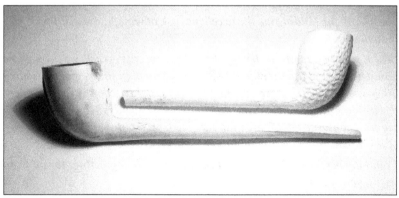

Typical 18th-century clay pipes. They were easily broken,
and became stained and darkened with use

Erbauliche Gedanken eines Tobackrauchers
Edifying Thoughts of a Tobacco Smoker

Sooft ich meine Tobackspfeife,
Mit gutem Knaster angefüllt,
Zur Lust und Zeitvertreib ergreife,
So gibt sie mir ein Trauerbild -
Und füget diese Lehre bei,
Dass ich derselben ähnlich sei.

Die Pfeife stammt von Ton und Erde,
Auch ich bin gleichfalls draus gemacht.
Auch ich muss einst zur Erde werden.
Sie fällt und bricht, eh ihr's gedacht,
Mir oftmals in der Hand entzwei.
Mein Schicksal ist auch einerlei.

Die Pfeife pflegt man nicht zu färben,
Sie bleibet weiß. Also der Schluss,
Dass ich auch dermaleinst im Sterben
Dem Leibe nach erblassen muss.
Im Grabe wird der Körper auch
So schwarz wie sie nach langem Brauch.

Wenn nun die Pfeife angezündet,
So sieht man, wie im Augenblick
Der Rauch in freier Luft verschwindet,
Nichts als die Asche bleibt zurück.
So wird des Menschen Ruhm verzehrt
Und dessen Leib in Staub verkehrt.

Wie oft geschieht's nicht bei dem Rauchen,
Dass, wenn der Stopfer nicht zur Hand,
Man pflegt den Finger zu gebrauchen.
Dann denk ich, wenn ich mich verbrannt:
O, macht die Kohle solche Pein,
Wie heiß mag erst die Hölle sein?

Ich kann bei so gestalten Sachen
Mir bei dem Toback jederzeit
Erbauliche Gedanken machen.
Drum schmauch ich voll Zufriedenheit
Zu Land, zu Wasser und zu Haus
Mein Pfeifchen stets in Andacht aus.

Every time I reach for my pipe,
Filled with good tobacco,
For pleasure or to pass the time,
The same sad thought comes to me -
And leads me to the conclusion
That I am quite similar to my pipe.

My pipe is made of clay and earth,
And I'm made of those things, too.
I, too, will one day be earth again.
Sometimes without warning it drops
From my hand and breaks in pieces.
My destiny is just the same.

One tries to keep the pipe pristine
And white. At the end of my life,
When I lay dying,
I, too, will become pale.
In the grave, my body will
Become as black as a well-used pipe.

When the pipe is burning,
One sees, in the wink of an eye,
How the smoke vanishes into thin air,
Leaving nothing behind but ash.
So will our earthly glory vanish
And our bodies turn to dust.

It often happens, when smoking,
That my pipe tool is not at hand,
So I tamp the tobacco with my finger.
If I burn my fingertip, I ask myself:
If glowing embers hurt so much,
How hot are the fires of Hell?

In contemplations such as these
With my tobacco, I always
Have edifying thoughts.
And so, filled with contentment,
On land, on sea, and at home,
I reverently puff on my pipe.

In the southeast corner of Leipzig's market square today there is a large elegant building known as the Königshaus (the King's House). The oldest structure on the square, it was built in 1538 and remodeled in Baroque style in the early 1700s. For several centuries, the Königshaus served as a residence for visiting dignitaries including the Electors of Saxony, Frederick the Great of Prussia, Napoléon Bonaparte, and the Russian Czar Peter the Great. Within its walls, conversations have taken place and deals made that changed the world.

Today it is no longer the house of kings: the building was converted into commercial space in 1904 and now houses upscale boutiques. In recent decades its exterior has been beautifully restored to colorful Baroque splendor, but virtually nothing remains of the original interior. An 18th-century engraving is shown on page 101.

Royal Night Music
The Great Light Show of 1734

In early October 1734, His Most Serene Highness, Frederick Augustus II, Prince and Elector of Saxony, travelled from his palace in Dresden to Leipzig to be adored by his subjects on the first anniversary of his coronation, and they did not let him down. On October 5, all of Leipzig and its environs honored Augustus with an outdoor lightshow and musical extravaganza.

The main feature of the event was a 30-minute cantata for choir, full orchestra and vocal soloists, composed by Bach especially for this occasion: *Preise dein Glücke, gesegnetes Sachsen (Celebrate your good fortune, blessed Saxony)* BWV 215.

Bach wrote the entire piece just a few days prior to the royal visit. While completing the score—and as his family and assistants copied the parts for the players and singers—Bach paid Leipzig publisher Breitkopf to print 700 booklets containing the text. That number was equal to more than 2% of the entire population of the city.

The Spectacle (*das Spektakel*)

The royal family ate their afternoon meal at the Königshaus, their residence while in Leipzig. At dusk the oil lamp streetlights were prepared and lit throughout the city. Then, at 7:00pm, just as the sun disappeared below the horizon, a cannon was fired as a signal and, according to the Leipzig *Town Chronicle,* the "entire town" was illuminated. The City Hall, adjacent to the Königshaus, was "magnificently decorated with many kinds of lamps," and the lights in the belfries of the St. Thomas and St. Nicholas churches could be seen for miles into the country. There is no balcony in the Königshaus, and the royal family observed the entire evening from the windows on the second or third floor.

The "many kinds of lamps" being used at that moment would have included large beeswax candles, open dish oil lamps, and torches fueled by animal fat, beeswax, or wood. Hundreds of people were needed to prepare, set up, light, and carefully manage these devices for as long as they continued to burn. It was a spectacular city-wide light show that lasted until midnight, and some of the devices were still burning early the next morning.

People came from far and wide to see the spectacle, and tickets were sold, but gate crashers made their way in as well, and thousands of people crowded the streets. There were no restroom facilities, but happily for everyone a waste and refuse gutter ran south through the main market square and right in front of the illuminated city hall. Then it turned right and passed between the royal residence and the serenading musicians. Much of the channel was boarded over for the event, but sections were left uncovered for the convenience of the crowd. (See the illustration on the following page.)

The scene of the 1734 outdoor concert and light show.

Opposite page: A detailed overhead view of the Central Market Place in Leipzig. The building with the tower on the opposite side of the plaza is the city hall. To the right of the city hall is the Königshaus. *(1712)*

This page: The view from the Königshaus windows looking north. The City Hall is on the right. *(Early 1700s)*

Als der

Allerdurchlauchtigste, Großmächtigste-
Fürst und Herr,

HERR

Friedrich August,

König in Pohlen und Groß-Hertzog von Litthauen,
Reußen, Preußen, Mazovien, Samogitien, Kiovien, Volhy-
nien, Podolien, Podlachien, Liefland, Smolensko, Severien und Czernicovien, ec. ec.
Hertzog zu Sachsen, Jülich, Cleve und Berg, auch Engern und Westphalen,
des Heil. Röm. Reichs Ertz-Marschall und Churfürst, Landgraf in Thüringen,
Marggraf zu Meissen, auch Ober- und Nieder-Lausitz, Burggraf zu Magdeburg,
Gefürsteter Graf zu Henneberg, Graf zu der Marck, Ravensberg und Barby,
Herr zu Ravensstein, ec. ec.

Nebst

Dero Allerdurchlauchtigsten

Gemahlin

mit Ihrer allerhöchsten Gegenwart die Stadt Leipzig
an der Michaelis-Messe 1734. beglückten,

Wolten

am 5ten October, als am Tage, an welchem

Ihro Majestät

im verwichenen 1733 ten Jahre

zum

König in Pohlen und Groß-Hertzog von Litthauen

gewehlet worden,

durch eine Abend-Music

ihre allerunterthänigste Devotion bezeigen

Die auf dasiger Universität Studirende.

The text booklet printed and distributed by Bach featured a memorable cover, shown on the opposite page. The top half of the cover is basically the colorful job description of Prince-Elector Frederick Augustus:

His most serene royal highness, the most mighty
Prince and Lord
by the grace of God
Frederick Augustus,
King of Poland and Grand Duke of Lithuania,
Reuss, Prussia, Mazovia, Samogitia, Kiovia, Volhynia,
Podolia, Podlachia, Liefland, Smolensko, Severia and Czernicovia, etc etc,
Duke of Saxony, Julich, Cleve and Berg, also Engern and Westphalia,
Archmarshall and Elector of the Holy Roman Empire, Landrave of Thuringia,
Margrave of Meissen, also Upper and Lower Lausitz, Burggrave of Magdeburg,
Prince and Count of Henneberg, Count of the Marck, Ravensberg and Barby,
Lord of Ravenstein, etc etc

The text continues with a mention of the Prince's wife (*Gemahlin*) and his coronation the year before, and concludes at the bottom of the page:

the students of the University of Leipzig wish to demonstrate
their most submissive devotion with an evening serenade.

The Music (*die Musik*)

The music began at 9:00pm with an entrance march accompanied by brass and drums as the cantata performers readied themselves in front of the Königshaus. The following report appeared in the Leipzig *Chronicle* several days later. ("Trumpets and drums" refers to the cantata, not the entrance march.)

At nine o'clock in the evening the students of Leipzig University presented His Majesty Prince Frederick Augustus with a most submissive evening serenade with trumpets and drums, composed by the honorable Kapellmeister Johann Sebastian Bach, Director of Music at St. Thomas School. A procession of all the musicians, with six hundred students carrying wax lights, made its way to the King's residence, where a special book containing the text of the serenade was presented to their Royal Majesties.

The cantata is an enormous composition, scored for three trumpets, 2 oboes, 2 flutes, violins, violas, cellos, double bass, keyboard and tympani. The 8-part choral movements that open and close the work are among the most complex of all Bach's cantatas, and they frame a series of seven inner movements for soprano, tenor and baritone soloists.

The singers were mostly university students. The orchestra was made up of Bach's Collegium Musicum players (fine players, many of whom were also university students), plus members of Leipzig's *Stadtpfeiffer* Guild (*town pipers*, e.g. wind and brass players) and *Kunstgeiger* Guild (*art fiddlers*, e.g. string players). Cantata 215 is a difficult work to perform in the best of situations, but Bach's performers would have been under-rehearsed and overwhelmed performing such a complex work outdoors in October by torchlight. However, the cantata is a joyous celebratory work, and the Elector and his family remained at the window until the end. The Chronicle reports that they were "heartily pleased" (*herzlich wohlgefallen*).

According to the newspaper report above, there were 600 torches fueled with beeswax, not to mention the lights described on the buildings around the square. This amount of beeswax was a phenomenal expense for the city, and it fueled an enormous number of torches, but the light was still feeble.

The torches were most likely some variety of cresset torch: a pole topped with a small concave container, bowl, or cage containing a combination of beeswax, rags, animal fat, wood, pine resin, or whatever else would burn. (See page 65.)

The choir and orchestra were positioned in front of the Königshaus at the south end of the market square, and they had a special need for light. Dozens of musicians were crowded together trying to read from parts hastily copied for them by Bach, his family, and his assistants. (Keep in mind the speed with which these parts were hand copied: Bach wrote the cantata in several days.)

One year before the event described on these pages, a similar event took place in the afternoon to celebrate the coronation of Augustus II. The Königshause is at the far end of the square on the left. To the left of the Königshaus is the tower of the city hall.

This entire event could easily have happened on a sunny afternoon with a lot less trouble and expense, but the newly developing possibilities for illuminated nighttime events were being exploited by royalty and regional authorities eager to enhance their "most mighty" image by creating a grand and otherworldly theatrical effect. It was also important for Leipzig to impress the Prince with the enthusiasm and adoration of its citizens. The hundreds of torches must have cast a flickering, magical glow on the facade of the Königshaus, and on the faces of the royal family looking down from the windows.

The Smoke (*der Rauch*)

The torches may have given off an undependable light, but they could be relied upon to produce prodigious amounts of sooty smoke that did not rise into the air but settled on everyone in the plaza.

The solo trumpeter in this performance was the eminent Gottfried Reiche, Bach's principal trumpeter and one of the leading town musicians. Bach was no doubt planning to engage him for the premiere of the *Christmas Oratorio* in ten weeks time. But on the morning after the royal concert, Reiche collapsed in front of his house and died of a stroke. He was 67. The *Chronicle* reported:

> *And this came about because he suffered great strains from playing on the previous day at the royal music, and the smoke from the torches had caused him much discomfort.*

Bach was involved in other outdoor and nighttime events, but this was the only one of his concerts from which a musician is known to have died.

As an employee of the city, Bach received extra pay for extra work. A signed receipt in the Leipzig archives is dated October 14, 1734, one week after the evening spectacle in front of the Königshaus. The sum of fifty Talers equals about 7% of Bach's total annual income from all sources in Leipzig.

> *That there has been duly paid to me, the undersigned, by the Registrar, 50 Taler, that is fifty thaler, for the production of the music recently offered to His Royal Majesty. Receipt is hereby acknowledged and gratefully given.*
>
> *{Signed} Joh. Seb. Bach*
>
> *Director of Choral Music and Cantor at St. Thomas Church*

Postscript:

Bach, ever the efficient composer, often borrowed from himself. He reused an aria from this cantata in his upcoming *Christmas Oratorio*, and re-used the music of the opening chorus for the *Osanna* in his *Mass in B Minor*. Other than those two recycled movements, this wonderful cantata was not performed again for more than a century. That's why Bach could reuse his music so freely: it was unpublished, and once he had performed it there was no assurance it would ever be heard again.

Above: The Königshaus in the 1720s. Compare with the recent photo on page 92.

Opposite: In an anonymous 1727 engraving, Leipzig students serenade a young lady who can be seen peeking out the window on the left. A small group of instrumentalists accompanies a bewigged man who holds a sheet of music and sings. Two students hold torches while other students and townspeople look on.

Medicine in the 18th Century:

In 1628 William Harvey published his discovery of the circulation of blood in the body.

In the late 1600s a microscope was built that was strong enough to see germs. Scientists were fascinated by the tiny wiggling things, but had no idea what they were.

There were no real doctors in any modern sense.

That's about it.

Meanwhile, there was:

no understanding of the causes of disease

no awareness of germs or pathogens

no hand washing before treatments, childbirth or surgery

no sterilization of medical instruments

no anesthetics, antibiotics, or antiseptics

Medicine and Mortality

Healing Arts (*Heilkunde*)

On the opposite page is a list of things people did not know. But what they thought they knew was just as much of a problem. The European theory of disease had been handed down from the Roman occupiers and was derived from the ancient theories of the Greek father of medicine himself, Hippocrates.

1. The body has four "humours" which must be kept in balance.

2. The four bodily humours are blood, phlegm, yellow bile, and black bile.

3. Diseases are spread by an invisible substance called miasma.

4. Disease is accompanied by an imbalance in the four humours.

7. The four humours were also related to the basic elements—Air, Water, Fire, and Earth—and all bodily fluids were thought to consist of combinations of these elements.

People were not sure if the humour imbalance caused the disease, or vice versa, but everyone agreed that diseases could be cured if the balance of the humours could be restored. Each of the four humours was associated with its own temperament (see illustration opposite).

This Iron Age theory of humors was the core of medical science, and even when following the theory made things worse, people still persisted in basing life and death decisions on it.

Bloodletting was one of these bad decisions. Because of the theory of the four humors, bloodletting was a frighteningly widespread medical treatment because eliminating an "overbalance" of blood could restore health. The draining of blood from sick people was accomplished either by cutting a vein with a razor and collecting the blood a bowl, or by placing leeches at certain points on the patient's body. Acutely ill patients (like Bach in his final year) who were subjected to bloodletting often expired sooner.

So where were the doctors?

The Barber-Surgeon (*der Bader, der Wundartzt*)

Until the beginning of the second millennium CE, most medical care was dispensed by the clergy. But concern arose about the propriety of priests causing the shedding of blood, and in 1163 it was declared sacrilegious for the clergy to draw blood from the human body. Although the priests were the only physicians, the church had effectively decreed that physicians could not be surgeons. Physician/priests could heal and administer remedies, but they could no longer cut.

Opposite: The four humors, from *The Book of Alchemy* by Leonard Thurneisser (1531-1596), physician to the court of Brandenburg. Published in Leipzig, 1574.

The sick and injured continued to seek medical help in the monasteries, because there was nowhere else to go. There, they began to entrust themselves to the care of the monastery barber and his razors. The priests with medical experience no doubt guided the barbers at first, but eventually the "barber-surgeons" began practicing outside the monasteries and became particularly popular during times of war.

A barber-surgeon was a "wound doctor" (*Bader* or *Wundartzt*)—a versatile practitioner of tooth extraction, enemas, bloodletting and wound surgery. Being a surgeon required no formal training at university. One "qualified" after an apprenticeship of a few years with another surgeon. Beginning in the 18th century, standards were imposed for the training of surgeons, and the "trade" was gradually elevated to the level of a profession. By the end of the century barbers could no longer be surgeons, and the dark age of medicine was coming to an end.

Mortality (*Sterblichkeit*)

Given the state of the healing arts described just above, it is easy to understand why death was a familiar visitor to families in the 18th century. Estimates of these things vary greatly, but an average of all the expert opinions suggests that in 18th-century Europe, only 10% of the population died of old age or "natural causes." The other 90% died before their time from accidents or from diseases that today would be curable.

Child and Maternal Mortality

In the 18th century (and in the 19th as well) nearly every parent experienced the death of at least one young child, and many lost spouses as well.

In Bach's time, nearly a quarter of all babies died before their first birthday. Fewer than half lived to be ten years old. As a result, women gave birth to as many children as possible, routinely six or eight and often more. Anna Magdalena Bach gave birth to 13 children in 19 years, and only six of them lived to adulthood.

Childbirth also presented serious hazards to the mother. In the early 1700s, there were *1,000 to 1,200 maternal deaths per 100,000 births*. And the more children, the higher the statistical likelihood that the mother would die in the process. In the modern industrial world, the rate of maternal death in childbirth is *16–20 maternal deaths per 100,000 births*.

The common attitude of indifference to young children was in some ways a reaction to the appalling infant mortality rate. Learned authorities advised parents not to become overly attached to their very young children. Physicians, such as they were at that time, were often less inclined to treat children for diseases, believing that once a disease had appeared, nothing could be done, and in any event it was only a child.

Edward Gibbon (b.1737), author of *The Decline and Fall of the Roman Empire*, suggested in his memoirs that

> ...*the death of a new born child before that of his parents may seem unnatural but it is a strictly probable event, since of any given number the greater part are extinguished* **before the ninth year, before they possess the faculties of the mind and the body.** [Emphasis added]

Gibbon's father, also called Edward, named all his male children Edward in the hope that one of them might survive and carry on the first name. Edward the author was the eldest child and the only sibling who survived. Five brothers and one sister born after him all died in infancy.

Maria Barbara Bach Dies Alone

Johann Sebastian Bach was well-acquainted with death, and with a life of grieving. The fact that Bach still was able to give to the world such an array of clear, transparent, uplifting and consoling music is a powerful testament to the stamina of the human spirit.

He was nine years old when both his parents died. He was 37 when his brother Jacob, the person with whom he was closest, died. Of his 20 children, ten died in childhood, and an eleventh died of illness in his 20s. And he was unable to say farewell to his first wife Maria Barbara, who died suddenly while he was away from home. One of the sad mysteries in this story is the unknown cause of her premature death.

In 1720, the 35-year-old Bach was Kapellmeister for Prince Leopold of Anhalt-Köthen. He and Maria Barbara had been happily married for 13 years, and they had a daughter and three sons ages eleven, nine, six and five.

For eight weeks in the summer Bach and six musicians accompanied the Prince and the royal entourage to the spa/resort of Baden. This was the second summer in which Maria Barbara remained at home with their four children.

In mid-summer an urgent message was sent to Bach from his home, but the Prince's staff intercepted it and told Bach nothing. After all, it would not do to inconvenience Prince Leopold by giving the Kappelmeister some reason to go home. Bach's son Carl Philipp Emanuel was the six-year-old mentioned above, and many years later he recalled the heart-rending scene:

> *The misfortune overtook my father, upon his return home from the journey to Carlsbad with his Prince, of finding his wife dead and buried, although he had left her healthy and hearty on his departure. He first received the news that she had become ill and died when he entered his home on his return.* (from 1750 obituary written in collaboration with J.F. Agricola)

Schlummert ein, ihr matten Augen, fallet sanft und selig zu.
(Fall asleep, you weary eyes, close gently and blessedly.)

– from the solo cantata *Ich habe genug*, BWV 82

The Children Who Died

Only ten of Bach's twenty children lived to be adults. Let us take a moment to consider the other ten, whose names are nearly forgotten today.

Note that seven of these ten deaths occurred in the seven years between 1726 and 1733. (The numbers indicate the child's place in the chronology of the twenty children.)

with Maria Barbara Bach
October 20, 1684–July 7, 1720
Married October 17, 1707

Twins:
3. Maria Sophia
February 23–March 15, 1713

4. Johann Christoph
Died at birth February 23, 1713

7. Leopold Augustus
November 15, 1718–September 28, 1719

with Anna Magdalena Wilcke
September 22 1701–February 22, 1760
Married December 3, 1721

8. Christiana Sophia Henrietta
Spring 1723–June 29, 1726

10. Christian Gottlieb
April 14, 1725–September 21, 1728

12. Ernestus Andreas
October 30–November 1, 1727

13. Regina Johanna
Oct 10, 1728–April 25, 1733

14. Christiana Benedicta
January 1–4, 1730

15. Christiana Dorothea
March 18, 1731–August 31, 1732

17. Johann August Abraham
November 5–6, 1733

The 1614 baptismal font in the altar of the St. Thomas Church. Eleven Bach children were baptized here. For a complete chronology of all twenty children, see page 36.

Bach's final years were filled with illness. He had cataracts, may have suffered from adult onset diabetes, and apparently had more than one stroke in the year of his death.

On March 28, 1750, a week after his 65th birthday, Bach underwent a brutal and primitive cataract operation carried out by a travelling English "eye physician." It was unsuccessful, and the procedure was repeated several weeks later. Both attempts failed, and Bach was blind. (The same physician used the same procedure on Handel in London a few years later, with the same results.)

Bach, already ill, was traumatized by the crude operation and the followup treatments which included bloodletting. After three months of blindness, pain and uncertainty, he had a stroke in mid July. A fever developed, and he deteriorated quickly, but until the day he died he was occupied with music. An assistant sat beside him as Bach—his eyes wrapped in bandages—lay in bed and discussed edits to the chorale *Vor deinen Thron tret ich hiermit (Before your throne I now appear)*. Soon after Bach's death, Carl Philipp Emanuel published his father's final composition, *The Art of the Fugue*, and this chorale was appended to it.

Johann Sebastian Bach died on July 28, 1750 at 8:15 in the evening. Three days later he was laid to rest in the cemetery of the St. John Church, and the following announcement was read from the pulpit of the St. Thomas Church:

> *Peacefully and blissfully departed in God the esteemed and highly respected Mr. Johann Sebastian Bach, Court Composer to His Royal Highness in Saxony, formerly Kapellmeister to the prince of Köthen and lately Director of Music of St. Thomas School. His dead body was this day, in accordance with Christian usage, committed to the earth.*

The family did not erect a headstone, and within a few generations the exact location of Bach's grave was forgotten.

Aside from his few published keyboard compositions, or an occasional unaccompanied choral motet in St. Thomas, no music by Johann Sebastian Bach would be heard again by the general public until eighty years after his death.

Under the poorest material conditions, without becoming discouraged by setbacks in his life and career, without publishing his music or appealing to the world to take notice of his work, his single concern was to create that which is true.

– Albert Schweitzer
(from his biography of Bach)

Johann Sebastian Bach

Born March 21, 1685, Eisenach
Died July 28, 1750, Leipzig

Ich freue mich auf meinen Tod,
Ach, hätt' er sich schon eingefunden.
Da entkomm ich aller Not,
Die mich noch auf der Welt gebunden.

I happily look forward to my death,
Ah, if only it had already found me.
There I shall escape from all the suffering
that continues to bind me to this world.

Text from the baritone solo cantata *Ich habe genug*, BWV 82,
premiered on February 2, 1727 in St. Thomas Church.

The grave of Johann Sebastian Bach in the St. Thomas Church.
His remains were interred here in 1950

Anna Magdalena Wilcke Bach

Born September 22, 1701, Weissenfels
Married Bach on December 3, 1721, Köthen
Died February 22, 1760, Leipzig

Anna Magdalena Wilcke was the daughter of a trumpeter in the town musicians of Weissenfels, a village 50 miles south of Köthen. She was a trained musician with a fine soprano voice, and it is thought that Bach met her when he hired soloists for concerts at the Köthen Court c.1720. When she and Johann Sebastian were married in 1721, she was 20 and he was a 36-year-old widower with four children. They had thirteen children of their own, and had been married for 28 years when he died in 1750. She was 49 at that time, and she outlived her husband by nearly a decade.

At the time of Bach's death, Anna Magdalena had little money, but found the funds to buy an expensive oaken casket for her husband's burial. His grave, however, was unmarked.

At the time of Bach's death, he and Anna Magdalena still had three minor children living at home: Regina Susanna (8) Johanna Carolina (13), and Johann Christian (15). The widow and children were legally entitled to live in the St. Thomas apartment for six months after Bach's death, but the city offered her a cash payment to vacate and she accepted.

Bach left no will, and Anna Magdalena received 1/3 of his estate. The remainder was distributed among the (male) children. The material received by Anna Magdalena included the manuscripts and performing parts for all the cantatas, which she sold to the school in return for a small payment.

After Bach's estate was settled, and his possessions had been distributed among the family members, Anna Magdalena and the two young daughters moved into a small apartment a few blocks away.

Johann Christian (15) was sent to live with his older half brother Carl Philipp Emanuel in Berlin.

Catharina Dorothea (42), the oldest surviving child of Bach and his first wife, had been a member of the Bach household all her life, and was only seven years younger than her stepmother, Anna Magdalena. After Bach's death, Catharina Dorothea went to live with her younger brother, Wilhelm Friedemann in Halle.

The City Council in its wisdom noticed that when Bach first began his Leipzig job, he had actually reported for work several weeks after the starting date stipulated in the contract. Since he had received payment in 1723 for days he didn't work, the City Council now—27 years later—deducted the overpayment from the pension funds owed to Bach's widow. That single payment was the only "pension" she received from the City Council.

Anna Magdalena received little other assistance. To her stepsons Carl Philpp Emanuel and Wilhelm Friedemann—who were financially able to help—she was the young girl their father had married after their mother died, and they had never accepted her into the family. To make matters worse, the city pension agreement forced Anna Magdalena to promise not to remarry. If she did remarry, she would forfeit legal custody of her underage children. This bizarre restriction insured that she and the two daughters who remained with her would live in poverty.

On May 19, 1752, nearly two years after Bach's death, the City Council paid Anna Magdalena 40 Taler, "in view of her poverty." The payment also covered the purchase of "certain pieces of music" by her late husband (several copies of *The Art of the Fugue*, published the year before). The sum of 40 Taler was the equivalent of 40% of Bach's base salary from the city, a fairly generous amount, and is an indication of the respect the council had for his memory. But that money ran out, there was no support from family, and she lived on welfare stipends given by the city to the indigent.

On February 27, 1760, at the age of 58, Anna Magdalena Wilcke Bach died in her small apartment on the Hainerstrasse, not far from her former home at the St. Thomas School. She was listed in the burial registry as a woman receiving charity (*Almösenfrau*), and was buried in a pine coffin at the St. John Church, the same cemetery where her husband was buried. No marker was erected.

A small group from the St. Thomas Boys' Choir sang at her burial, not because she was the wife of J.S. Bach but because it was the choir's job to sing at funerals at that cemetery. The record states that "1/5 choir" was present, meaning a few of the youngest boys sang hymns led by an older student. The choir fee was paid by the family of the deceased, who in fact received a discount because of the connection to the former Thomas Cantor.

A Song of Farewell

In 1725, two years after they moved to Leipzig, Anna Magdalena and her husband began compiling their second "notebook," a private, hand-written collection of enjoyable pieces (by Bach and many others) for home music-making. The notebook includes a song from a 1718 opera by Gottfried Stölzel—a tender opera aria, not a religious song. In the original notebook, the melody and the lyrics are in Anna Magdalena's handwriting, and the harmony has been filled in by Bach.

Bist du bei mir, geh' ich mit Freuden	*If you are with me, I will go gladly*
zum Sterben und zu meiner Ruh'.	*to my death and to my rest.*
Ach, wie vergnügt wär' so mein Ende,	*Ah, how pleasant would be my end,*
es drückten deine lieben Hände	*if your dear hands would*
mir die getreuen Augen zu!	*close my faithful eyes!*

The Children

Seven of Anna Magdalena's own children preceded her in death. She was survived by six children and three stepchildren. Gottfried Heinrich (mentally disabled) died in 1863, age 38. Catharina Dorothea—the oldest Bach child—died in 1774, age 66, and Johanna Carolina in 1781, age 43; both were unmarried. A widowed daughter, Liesl Bach Altnikol, returned to Leipzig and died there in 1781, age 55. The composer brothers followed in death: Johann Christian (1782, age 46), Wilhelm Friedemann (1784, age 73), Carl Philipp Emanuel (1788, age 74), and Johann Christoph Friedrich (1795, age 62).

The last of Bach's children to die was the youngest: Regina Susanna, born in Leipzig in 1742. After her siblings were gone, she was alone living on charity, and her condition became wretched. In 1800, a call went out in a German musical publication for donations to the daughter of "the great Sebastian Bach," and a modest sum was collected on her behalf by a Leipzig music publisher. Regina Susanna Bach—the last of Bach's children—died in 1809 at the age of 67.

The Legacy of Anna Magdalena

In 1894, an attempt was made to locate Bach's grave in the cemetery of the St. John Church. Local lore maintained that he had been buried "six paces" from the south portal of the church, and in fact an oaken coffin containing the skeleton of a man was among those found in that vicinity. The bones were examined by an anatomist who measured the ear openings in the skull and concluded that the individual would have had excellent hearing. Scholars decided that these must be the remains of J. S. Bach, but no further tests were made and no proof has ever been offered.

The same scholars in 1894 hoped that Anna Magdalena and her husband might have shared a double grave, with her casket buried atop his. Adjacent to the grave they believed to be Bach's, researchers did indeed find fragments of a pine coffin and the bones of a woman, along with a delicate silver wedding ring and a silver thimble. The remains thought to be Bach's were reinterred inside the sanctuary of St. John, but the female remains were returned to the grave in the cemetery.

Until the 1940s, the ring and thimble were exhibited in St. John Church as items believed to have belonged to Anna Magdalena Bach, but the church and cemetery were nearly destroyed by bombs during World War II, and the ring and thimble were lost. Bach's safely entombed remains were moved from the St. John sanctuary to the altar of St. Thomas Church in 1950, but the location—or even existence—of Anna Magdalena's grave is unknown.

We have no portrait of Anna Magdalena Bach but her handwriting is well-known to musicologists from the manuscripts and scores she copied for her husband during their three decades together. Without her devotion to him and her involvement in his life, the history of music might have been quite different.

A pastel believed to be of of Bach, possibly made after his death. It is thought to be by Gottlieb Friedrich Bach or his son Johann Philipp Bach, distant cousins in the Meiningen branch of the Bach family tree.

Epilogue

In the face of such shape and weight of present misfortune, the voice of the individual artist may seem perhaps of no more consequence than the whirring of a cricket in the grass, but the arts do live continuously, and they live literally by faith; their names and their shapes and their uses and their basic meanings survive unchanged in all that matters through times of interruption, diminishment, neglect; they outlive governments and creeds and the societies, even the very civilization that produced them. They cannot be destroyed altogether because they represent the substance of faith and the only reality. They are what we find again when the ruins are cleared away.

~ Katherine Anne Porter, 1940

In 1908 this statue of Johann Sebastian Bach by Leipzig sculptor
Carl Seffner was erected in the courtyard of the St. Thomas Church.

Appendix

MODERN
GERMANY

Baltic Sea

DENMARK

North Sea

SCHLESWIG-
HOLSTEIN

Lübeck •

MECKLENBURG-
VORPOMMERN

• Schwerin

HAMBURG•

BREMEN

Lüneburg•

BRANDENBURG

POLAND

NIEDERSACHSEN
(LOWER SAXONY)

NETHERLANDS

• Hannover

SACHSEN-
ANHALT

BERLIN

Potsdam

NORDRHEIN-
WESTFALEN

Köthen •

Halle •

Leipzig

THÜRINGEN
(THURINGIA)

• Mühlhausen

SACHSEN (SAXONY)

Kassel •

Arnstadt •

• Weimar

Dresden

Eisenach •

• Ohrdruf

• Köln

HESSE

BELGIUM

RHEINLAND-
PFALZ

Frankfurt
•

CZECH REPUBLIC
(BOHEMIA)

•
Prague

LUXEMBOURG

SAARLAND

• Nürenberg

BAYERN
(BAVARIA)

Stuttgart
•

FRANCE

BADEN-
WÜRTTEMBERG

• München

AUSTRIA

• Salzburg

SWITZERLAND

Miles   50   100   150

Modern Germany

The modern Federal Republic of Germany shown in these maps has 16 states including the cities of Bremen, Hamburg, and Berlin. However, until the mid 19th century the map was very fluid: at times the German Empire had more than two dozen independent states, duchies and principalities, and for a while it included most of Poland and the Czech Republic. The country we know today as Germany did not become a single entity until after 1848.

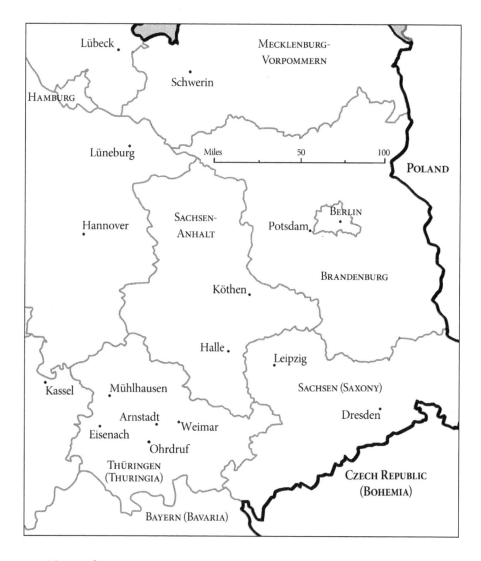

Bach's World

Bach was born in 1685 in the town of Eisenach in the province of Thuringia, a region where several generations of the Bach family had lived before him. Thuringia maintained a friendly cultural rivalry with Saxony, its neighbor to the east. Saxony revolved around two major urban centers of cultural activity: the courtly city of Dresden and the university city of Leipzig. Thuringia had more centers of cultural activity, but none was as large as the two Saxon cities.

Bach's geographical world was small, and he spent his life as an employee within the borders of Thuringia, Sachsen-Anhalt, and Saxony. The world he actually knew firsthand is easy to delineate by imagining a line connecting these cities: *Eisenach, Ohrdruf, Dresden, Berlin, Lüneburg, Kassel, Eisenach.* Other than a brief trip north to Lübeck when he was 20, Bach never travelled outside this perimeter.

J. S. Bach Timeline

Eisenach and Ohrdruf (1685–1700)

1685

March 21: Johann Sebastian is born in the town of Eisenach, the eighth child of trumpeter Johann Ambrosius Bach and Maria Elisabeth Bach. In that region there were so many professional musicians named Bach that "Bach" had become a synonym for musician.

1686

Death of his sister, age 6.

1690-92

Attends the German school in Eisenach.

1691

Death of his brother, age 14.

1692-95

Attends the Latin school in Eisenach.

1694

Spring: Death of his father's twin brother.

May: Death of his mother.

1695

February: Death of his father.

Baptismal font in the St. George Church in Eisenach. Bach was baptized here in March 1685.

Spring: Bach (age 10) and brother Johann Jacob (13) move into the household of their eldest brother, Johann Christoph Bach, organist in the town of Ohrdruf.

1695-1700

Attends the Lyceum Illustre Gleichense school in Ohrdruf.

Lüneburg and Weimar (1700–1703)

1700

March 15: With his school friend Georg Erdman, Bach journeys on foot from Ohrdruf to Lüneburg (roughly 200 miles). After auditioning for a boarding school there, he receives a scholarship because of his clear soprano singing voice. When his voice breaks, he maintains the scholarship with his violin playing. During these two years, he meets local and visiting professional musicians, and has access to a large music library.

1702

April: He leaves the Lüneburg school without graduating and returns to his home area around Eisenach and Ohrdruf.

July 9: He auditions successfully for the position of organist at the St. Jacob Church in Sängerhausen, but the job is given to a local.

1703

January–June: He is employed as a violinist in the ensemble at the court of Duke Johann Ernst of Saxe-Weimar.

Arnstadt (1703–1707)

July 13: He auditions on the newly-built organ at the St. Boniface Church in Arnstadt and accepts the job of organist. He is 18 years old, and will hold this job for four mostly uneventful years. (See photo on page 66.)

1705

November: He is given a four-week leave of absence to visit and study with Dieterich Buxtehude in Lübeck, but is absent from Arnstadt for nearly four months.

1706

February: The Arnstadt City Council is highly displeased and discusses disciplinary matters regarding Bach.

November 29: He auditions for a church in Langewiesen, but is not hired.

1707

June: After an audition and negotiations, Bach signs a contract for the organist position at St. Blasius Church in Mühlhausen.

June 29: Bach's Arnstadt contract officially ends, and he receives permission to leave Arnstadt.

Mühlhausen (1707–1708)

July 1: Bach begins work as organist at St. Blasius Church in Mühlhausen.

October 17: Bach marries his cousin Maria Barbara Bach in Dornheim, near Arnstadt. They would have seven children; four lived to maturity. From the town register:

"Mr. Johann Sebastian Bach, duly appointed organist at the Church of St. Blasius in the Imperial Free City of Mühlhausen, still single, youngest surviving son and lawful issue of the late Mr. Johann Ambrosius Bach, Musician to the Prince of Saxe-Eisenach, and Mistress Maria Barbara, youngest daughter and lawful issue of the late Master Johann Michael Bach, organist in Gehren, were united in marriage in Dornheim on October 17. The fees were remitted."

1708

February 4: The Cantata *Gott ist mein König (God is my King)*, BWV 71 is performed to celebrate the election of the Mühlhausen Town Council, and the cantata is printed and distributed. *This is the only choral composition by J. S. Bach to be published during his lifetime.*

June: Bach is offered the position of organist and chamber musician to co-reigning brothers, Dukes Wilhelm Ernst and Ernst August of Saxe-Weimar.

June 20: Bach's contract in Mühlhausen is officially ended and he is given permission to leave.

WEIMAR (1708-1717)

July 14: Bach and Maria Barbara move to Weimar.

Bach's annual salary in Weimar was 150 florins cash; 18 bushels of wheat; 12 bushels of barley; four cords of firewood; and 30 buckets of tax-free beer.

December 29: Birth of first child, Catharina Dorothea (d.1774).

1709

February 4: Guest performance of an unknown cantata at the Mühlhausen Town Council election.

1710

February 4: Another guest performance at Mühlhausen Town Council election.

October 26: Bach is hired to test a new organ in Traubach, near Weimar.

November 22: Birth of second child, Wilhelm Friedemann (d.1784).

1711

June 3: Bach receives a salary increase in Weimar.

1713

February 23: Birth of twins. One dies at birth, the other lives for two weeks.

October 21-22: For the birthday of Duke Christian of Saxe-Weissenfels, Bach leads a performance of Cantata BWV 208 in Weissenfels.

November 28 through December 15: Bach auditions successfully for the post of organist at Our Lady (Market) Church in Halle, but declines after getting a raise in Weimar.

1714

March 2: Appointed *Master of Concerts* at Weimar and receives a salary increase.

March 8: Birth of fifth child, Carl Philipp Emanuel (d.1788).

1715

May 11: Birth of sixth child, Johann Gottfried Bernhard (d.1739).

August 1–November 3: Official period of mourning after the death of Duke Wilhelm Ernst of Weimar.

1717

August 5: Bach signs a contract for the Kapellmeister position in Köthen, but had not yet received permission to leave the Weimar job.

October: Bach engages in a famous contest with French organist Louis Marchand in Dresden. Intimidated by Bach's reputation, Marchand left town before their appointed public meeting.

Nov 6–Dec 2: After months of dispute, Bach is jailed for 'too stubbornly' insisting on release from his Weimar service. He is finally dismissed (in disgrace) partly through the influence of the Prince of Köthen.

December 16-18: He tests a newly-built organ at the St. Paul (or "University") Church in Leipzig

KÖTHEN (1717-1723)

December 29: Bach and Maria Barbara arrive in Köthen with their four children.

1718

May–July: Bach and six court musicians travel to the resort of Carlsbad with Prince Leopold.

November 15: Birth of seventh child, Leopold Augustus. Prince Leopold is godfather. The child lives less than a year.

1719

March: Purchases a harpsichord for Köthen during a trip to Berlin where he meets the Margrave of Brandenburg, who asks Bach to send him some music.

June: Bach makes an unsuccessful attempt to meet Handel while in Halle.

1720

January 22: Publishes the *Clavier-Büchlein* (*Little Organ Book*), a collection of keyboard excercises originally written for his son Wilhelm Friedemann.

May–July: Bach and the court musicians again travel to Carlsbad with Prince Leopold. Messages sent to Bach from home are intercepted by courtiers. He arrives home in July to find that Maria Barbara has died, leaving Bach a widower with four young children.

November: Bach performs several auditions for the organ post at St. James Church in Hamburg, but withdraws.

1721

March 24: Bach sends a manuscript of six concertos "with several instruments" to Christian Ludwig, Margrave of Brandenburg.

December 3: Bach marries Anna Magdalena Wilcke, a professional soprano and the daughter of a musician in Weissenfels. She is 20, Bach is 36 and has four children, ages 13, 11, 7, and 6. They would have 13 children of their own; only 6 lived to maturity.

December 11: In a cruel twist of fate, Bach's employer, Prince Leopold of Köthen, marries a young noblewoman who does not care for Bach's style of music. His musical workload evaporates and the royal musical gatherings cease, although he maintains a cordial relationship with the Prince.

1722

Bach begins to compose and compile the contents of the first *Anna Magdalena Notebook*, and completes Book 1 of *The Well-Tempered Clavier*.

April 16: Death of his older brother, Johann Jacob, aged 40. Together they had survived being orphaned as children.

December 21: Bach writes an application for the position of Director of Music at St. Thomas School in Leipzig.

1723

Breitkopf music publishing house is established in Leipzig.

February 7: Bach conducts his audition for the Leipzig job.

Spring: Birth of eighth child, Sophia Henrietta. She lives for three years.

April 13: Bach's request for dismissal from Köthen is granted, but he retains the (non-resident) Kapellmeister title.

LEIPZIG (1723–1750)

May 5: Bach signs his contract with the Leipzig Town Council.

May 8: Bach undergoes a theological examination by two professors to confirm his adherence to Lutheran creed.

Mid May: The Bach family arrives in Leipzig in two coaches and with five wagons of possessions. Johann Sebastian is 38. Anna Magdalena is 22. They have five children, age 14, 12, 9, 8, and 2 months.

May 15: Bach receives his first Leipzig salary payment.

May 16: First performance as Music Director: Cantata BWV 59 at St. Paul Church (University Church).

May 30: Bach's first annual cycle of church cantatas begins. For the next several years, he writes an average of one cantata per week.

June 1: Bach's formal installation as Cantor of the St. Thomas School.

December: Bach premieres a *Magnificat* and a *Sanctus* in the Thomaskirche. In 1733 he would incorporate the *Sanctus* into the *Mass in B Minor*.

1724

February 27: Birth of ninth child, Gottfried Heinrich (d.1763).

April 7: First performance of the *St. John Passion*.

July 18: Guest performance in Köthen with Anna Magdalena.

1725 (age 40)

February: Guest performance of a cantata in Weissenfels.

March 30: Performance of a revised version of the *St. John Passion*.

April 14: Birth of tenth child, Christian Gottlieb. He lives for three years.

September 19-20: Organ recitals in Dresden.

December: Guest performances in Köthen with Anna Magdalena.

Leipzig Stock Exchange is established.

1726

April 5: Birth of eleventh child, Elisabeth Juliana Frederica ("Liesl" or "Liessgen") (d.1781).

June 29: Death of daughter Christiana Sophia Henrietta, aged three.

November 1: Announcement of the *Clavier-Übung* series (*Keyboard Studies*).

1727

The population of Leipzig reaches 30,000, an increase of 10,000 in one decade. It is one of the most important trade, publishing, and educational centers in Germany.

March through April: Partial renovation of St. Thomas School apartment.

April 11: First performance of the *St. Matthew Passion*.

October 17: Performance of Cantata BWV 198 at memorial service for Christiane Eberhardine, wife of Prince Augustus of Saxony.

October 30: Birth of 12th child, Ernestus Andreas. He lives for two days.

1728

September 21: Death of son, Christian Gottlieb, aged three.

October 10: Birth of 13th child, Regina Johanna. She lives 4 1/2 years.

November 19: Death of Bach's former employer, Prince Leopold of Köthen (age 33).

December 27: Death of sister, Marie Salome Bach Wiegand.

1729

January 5: Guest performance in Köthen.

January 12: Performance of Cantata BWV 210a during visit to Leipzig of Christian, Duke of Saxe-Weissenfels.

February: Guest performances in Weissenfels and appointment as honorary Kapellmeister of the Saxe-Weissenfels court.

March 20: Assumes the salaried directorship of the Collegium Musicum in their concert series at Zimmermann's coffeehouse.

Spring: Disputes escalate with the City Council over the admission of unmusical pupils to the St. Thomas School. Bach is losing control of the selection process.

March 23-24: Performance of Cantata BWV 244a at funeral service of Prince Leopold in Köthen.

April 15: Performance of the revised *St. Matthew Passion.*

June 29: Bach extends an invitation to Handel to visit Leipzig. It is not known if Handel replied, and illness prevents Bach from journeying to Halle. By that time, Handel was an English citizen living in London.

November: A new City Councilman takes control of St. Thomas School student applications. Bach can no longer choose the singers who will be in his choirs.

December 24: Bach auditions new organists for the post at St. Nicholas Church.

1730

January 1: Birth of fourteenth child, Christiana Benedicta. She lives for three days.

August 2: Dispute with the Town Council about teaching duties.

August 23: Bach sends to the Leipzig town council a now-famous written complaint about the musicians (vocal and instrumental) with whom he had to work in the Leipzig churches and the St. Thomas School. He goes on to make detailed suggestions for a more "well-appointed" church music ensemble.

October 28: Bach writes a letter to his childhood friend Georg Erdmann, in which he complains about his job and his salary, and says he is seeking possible employment elsewhere.

1731

March 18: Birth of fifteenth child, Christiana Dorothea. She lives for 17 months.

March 23: Performance of *St. Mark Passion*, BWV 247, on Good Friday.

Spring: Publication of *Clavier-Übung I*, BWV 825-30, as "Opus 1."

May: The Bach family relocates to temporary quarters during the rebuilding of the St. Thomas School building.

September 14: Organ recital at the St. Sophia Church in Dresden.

1732

April 24: The Bach family returns to their renovated residence in south wing of the St. Thomas School.

June 5: Performance of Cantata BWV Anh. 18 to open the school building.

June 21: Birth of sixteenth child, Johann Christoph Friedrich. Composer and church musician. (d.1795).

August 31: Death of daughter Christiana Dorothea, age 17 months.

September 2: Trip to Kassel with Anna Magdalena for organ examination at St. Martin Church.

1733

February 1: Death of Frederick Augustus I of Saxony (age 63). Born on May 2, 1670, he was known as *August der Starke* (*Augustus the Strong*). His son Frederick Augustus II will soon receive the crown. Bach writes a series of cantatas for the Prince's family during the coming year.

April 25: Death of daughter Regina Johanna, age 4 1/2 years.

June 23: Son, Wilhelm Friedemann (23), is appointed organist at Sophienkirche, Dresden.

July 27: Bach and Anna Magdalena visit Dresden to deliver the manuscript of a new Mass to the new Prince Frederick Augustus II. It is the two core movements of what is today known as the *Mass in B Minor*.

August 3: Bach begins a series of celebratory cantatas for the new Prince.

November 5: Birth of seventeenth child, Johann August Abraham. He lives only one day.

December 8: Performs the festive cantata *Tönet, ihr Pauken!*, BWV 214, to honor the 34th birthday of Maria Josepha, Queen of Poland and Electress of Saxony. The performance at Gottfried Zimmermann's coffee-house required one of the largest ensembles of any of Bach's cantatas: four vocal soloists; 4-part chorus; and an orchestra of 3 trumpets, timpani, 2 flutes, 2 oboes, oboe d'amore, continuo harpsichord, and full strings.

1734

January 17-19: Outdoor performance during Leipzig celebration of the coronation of Frederick Augustus II as King of Poland.

October 5: In an outdoor performance in the central market square of Leipzig, Bach and his city musicians perform a cantata for Prince Augustus, Elector of Saxony. The royal family observes the performance from the balcony. Bach's leading trumpeter Gottfried Reiche dies the following day of a stroke brought on by smoke inhalation.

December 25, 26, 27: First three cantatas of the *Christmas Oratorio* are premiered.

1735

January 1, 4, 6: The remaining cantatas of the *Christmas Oratorio* are premiered.

March 21: Bach's fiftieth birthday. Draws up an extensive history of the male musicians in his family.

Spring: Publication of *Clavier-Übung II*.

September 5: Birth of eighteenth child, Johann Christian ("Christel") (d.1782).

1736

March 30: Performance of further revised version of the *St. Matthew Passion*.

November 19: Bach is granted the honorary, non-resident post of Royal Saxon Court Composer (a title and a small stipend).

December: Organ recital at St. Mary Church in Dresden.

1737

October 30: Birth of nineteenth child, Johanna Carolina. (d.1781).

1738

May: In Dresden.

1739

May 27: Death of son Johann Gottfried Bernhard, aged 24.

August: Concerts in Dresden with lutenists Silvius Leopold Weiss and Johann Kropffgans.

Fall: Publication of *Clavier-Übung III*.

November: Visits Weissenfels with Anna Magdalena.

1740

April 17: Trip to Halle in another unsuccessful attempt to meet Handel.

1741

August: Trip to Berlin.

Fall: Publication of *Clavier-Übung IV*.

November: Extended trip to Dresden.

1742

February 22: Birth of twentieth child, Regina Susanna (d.1809).

August 30: Performance of the *Peasant Cantata*, BWV 212 for a civic celebration in Kleinzschocher, a Leipzig suburb.

1744

Spring: Five-week journey. Destination unknown.

1745

November 30: Birth of first grandchild, Johann Adam (son of Carl Philipp Emanuel).

1747

May 7: Meets with King Frederick II of Prussia in Potsdam.

May 8: Plays an organ recital in the Church of the Holy Spirit in Potsdam.

June: Becomes a member of the Society of Musical Science and contributes his *Canonic Variations*, BVW 769, for publication.

July 28: Start of major organ repairs at St. Thomas Church.

September: Publication of the *Musical Offering*, BWV 1079.

November: Examination of renovated organ at St. Thomas Church.

1749

April 4: Performance of *St. John Passion*.

Mid May: Sudden onset of serious illness and eye trouble, possibly involving a stroke or complications from diabetes. He is losing his sight to cataracts.

1750

March 28–31: Cataract surgery performed by Englishman Dr. John Taylor.

April 5–8: Second eye surgery. Both surgeries are failures.

July 22: Suffers a stroke and receives holy communion.

July 28: Dies at 8:15 in the evening.

July 31: Burial in the cemetery of the St. John Church. No headstone is erected.

November: After inventory, Bach's estate is divided among his wife and sons.

After Bach's Death

1750–1829

For 79 years, nearly all of Bach's music remains unpublished and unperformed. His few published keyboard works keep his reputation from fading. Learned musicians including Mozart and Beethoven play Bach's keyboard music, and strive to obtain handwritten copies of the major unpublished choral works.

1825

For his 16th birthday Felix Mendelssohn-Bartholdy's grandmother gives him a hand-copied manuscript of the *St. Matthew Passion*.

1829

Mendelssohn conducts a performance of the work in Berlin. For the first time since the 1740s, the world hears a performance of choral/orchestral music by Bach. This famous concert ignites the great 19th-century "Bach Revival."

1840s–1899

Musicologists begin searching for the surviving manuscripts from Bach's musical estate and gathering them at the Royal Library in Berlin. The first complete edition of Bach's works is compiled, edited, and published.

The west facade of the St. Thomas School with the church roof and steeple beyond. The photograph was taken in 1885, 135 years after Bach's death. In 1902 the building was demolished, despite the protests of historians.

Gratias agimus tibi
(We give thanks to you)
– from the *Gloria* of the Latin Mass

Words about J. S. Bach

Not "Brook" but "Ocean" should be his name.

– Ludwig van Beethoven (*Bach* is the German word for *stream* or *brook*)

Study Bach: there you will find everything.

– Johannes Brahms

The greatest music in the world... if life had taken hope and faith from me, this single chorus would restore all.

– Felix Mendelssohn

And if we look at the works of J.S. Bach—a benevolent god to which all musicians should offer a prayer to defend themselves against mediocrity—on each page we discover things which we thought were born only yesterday, from delightful arabesques to an overflowing of religious feeling greater than anything we have since discovered. And in his works we will search in vain for anything the least lacking in good taste.

– Claude Debussy

Now there is music from which a man can learn something.

– W. A. Mozart (on hearing Bach motets in the St. Thomas Church)

Bach is the beginning and end of all music.

– Max Reger

Bach is like an astronomer who, with the help of ciphers, finds the most wonderful stars.

– Frédéric Chopin

I had no idea of the historical evolution of the civilized world's music and had not realized that all modern music owes everything to Bach.

– Niccolai Rimsky-Korsakov

She played Bach. I do not know the names of the pieces, but I recognized the stiff ceremonial of the frenchified little German courts and the sober, thrifty comfort of the burghers, and the dancing on the village green, the green trees that looked like Christmas trees, and the sunlight on the wide German country, and a tender coziness; and in my nostrils there was a warm scent of the soil and I was conscious of a sturdy strength that seemed to have its roots deep in mother earth, and of an elemental power that was timeless and had no home in space.

– W. Somerset Maugham (from his short story "The Alien Corn")

Bach is thus a terminal point. Nothing comes from him; everything merely leads to him.

– Albert Schweitzer

O you happy sons of the North who have been reared at the bosom of Bach, how I envy you.

– Giuseppe Verdi

Bach is a colossus of Rhodes, beneath whom all musicians pass and will continue to pass. Mozart is the most beautiful, Rossini the most brilliant, but Bach is the most comprehensive: he has said all there is to say. If all the music written since Bach's time should be lost, it could be reconstructed on the foundation which Bach laid.

– Charles Gounod

...the most stupendous miracle in all music!

– Richard Wagner

In Bach the vital cells of music are united as the world is in God.

– Gustav Mahler

The poetry, the atmosphere, the intensity of expression, the beauty of the preludes and fugues grip, overwhelm, and stimulate us. Let us not be afraid of the supreme contrapuntal science of the fugues, nor be overawed by the stern appearance and heavy wig of Father Bach. Let us gather around him, feel the love, the noble goodness that flow from each one of his phrases and that invigorate and bind us by ties strong and warm.

– Carl Friedrich Zeltler (letter to Goethe, 9 June 1827)
    (Zelter introduced the young Felix Mendelssohn to Bach's music, and
    thereby brought about the great "Bach Revival" in the 19th century.)

Any musician, even the most gifted, takes a place second to Bach's at the very start.

– Paul Hindemith

If one were asked to name one musician who came closest to composing without human flaw, I suppose general consensus would choose Johann Sebastian Bach.

– Aaron Copland

Bach is the supreme genius of music... This man, who knows everything and feels everything, cannot write one note, however unimportant it may appear, which is anything but transcendent. He has reached the heart of every noble thought, and has done it in the most perfect way.

To strip human nature until its divine attributes are made clear, to inform ordinary activities with spiritual fervor, to give wings of eternity to that which is most ephemeral; to make divine things human and human things divine; such is Bach, the greatest and purest moment in music of all time.

– Pablo Casals

Postscript

A wide variety of earthly music, including some by Bach, was recorded onto a solid gold LP record and sent into the far reaches of outer space on the two Voyager Spacecraft in the 1970s. During the selection period, when the distinguished biologist and author Lewis Thomas was asked what music he would want sent into outer space to represent Earth, he replied, "I would send the complete works of Johann Sebastian Bach. But that would be boasting."

Glossary of German Titles of Nobility

Reigning titles are listed here in order of descending rank, followed by their English equivalents. German nobility (*deutscher Adel*) and its hereditary privileges were abolished by the Weimar Republic in 1919.

Kaiser, Kaiserin
Emperor, Empress

König, Königin
King, Queen

> **Prinz, Prinzessin** (a child of royal blood)
> Prince, Princess

> **Fürst, Fürstin** (a regional sovereign, see opposite page)
> Prince, Princess

Kurfürst, Kurfürstin
Prince-Elector, Princess-Electress

Erzherzog, Erzherzogin
Archduke, Archduchess

Grossherzog, Grossherzogin
Grand Duke, Grand Duchess

A prince could be outranked by an Archduke or a Grand Duke with royal blood.

Herzog, Herzogin
Duke, Duchess

Pfalzgraf, Pfalzgräfin
Count-Palatine, Countess-Palatine

Markgraf, Markgräfin
Margrave, Margravine, or Marquess, Marchioness

Landgraf, Landgräfin
Landgrave, Landgravine

Burggraf, Burggräfin
Burggrave, Burggravine

Graf, Gräfin
Earl/Count, Countess

Baron, Baronin; Freiherr, Freifrau
Baron, Baroness

Prinz/Prince or Fürst/Prince?

A common source of confusion in English translations is the use of the word *prince* in reference to two different German titles—*Prinz* and *Fürst*. These two German words exist in order to make an important distinction that does not appear in English:

1.) **Prinz**: The son of the King, of royal blood lineage.

2.) **Fürst**: A unique German title referring to a sovereign with total, direct and personal rule over a specific region but who is still under the rule of the Emperor or King. The English translation *Prince* is misleading, because a *Fürst* is not necessarily of royal lineage and can actually be outranked by several other titles further down the list on the opposite page.

3.) **Kurfürst**: In some cases a *Fürst* was also an *Elector of the Holy Roman Empire*. Until 1806, their "votes" gave official approval to the coronation in Vienna of the hereditary Emperors. An Elector's title was *Kurfürst*, literally "the prince who chooses," sometimes translated *Prince-Elector*.

The changing borders and politics of Europe could lead to intriguing and colorful combinations of titles, especially for the Prince-Electors of Saxony. See page 95 for the Kurfürst's magnificent list of titles in 1734.

Partial list of titled patrons for whom Bach composed and performed:

Johann Ernst III, Duke of Saxe-Weimar *(co-employer 1703 and 1708-1717)*

Wilhelm Ernst, Duke of Saxe-Weimar *(same)*

Leopold, Prince of Anhalt-Köthen *(employer 1717-1723)*

Christian Ludwig, Margrave of Brandenburg

Christian, Duke of Saxe-Weissenfels

Kurfürst Frederick Augustus I of Saxony (Augustus the Strong)

Princess Christiane Eberhardine of Brandenburg-Bayreuth, his wife

Kurfürst Frederick Augustus II of Saxony, their son

Archduchess Maria Josepha of Austria, his wife

Count Frantisek Antonin von Sporck of Bohemia

Count Hermann-Karl von Keyserling of Russia

Frederick, Landgrave of Hesse-Kassel and King of Sweden

Frederick, King of Prussia (Frederick the Great)

Further Reading

This is a careful selection of only the most valuable resources encountered by the author. Most of these books would fit into several of the categories below.

Books with particularly rich content.

J. S. Bach

* Eidam, Klaus. *The True Life of J.S. Bach.* New York: Basic, 2001.

* Gaines, James R. *Evening in the Palace of Reason: Bach Meets Frederick the Great in the Age of Enlightenment.* New York, NY: Fourth Estate, 2005.

* Gardiner, John Eliot. *Bach: Music in the Castle of Heaven.* New York: Knopf, 2013. Print and eBook.

Korth, Michael, and Stephan Kuhlmann. *J.S. Bach: Bilder und Zeugnisse eines Musikerlebens.* München: Artemis, 1985.

Harnoncourt, Nikolaus. "Bach and the Musicians of His Age" in *The Musical Dialogue.* Portland: Amadeus Press, 1984.

Petzoldt, Martin, and Joachim Petri. *Johann Sebastian Bach: Ehre sei dir Gott gesungen.* Göttingen: Vandenhoeck & Ruprecht, 1988.

* Wolff, Christoph. *Johann Sebastian Bach: The Learned Musician.* New York: W.W. Norton, 2000.

* Wolff, Christoph, Hans T. David, and Arthur Mendel. *The New Bach Reader: A Life of Johann Sebastian Bach in Letters and Documents.* New York: W.W. Norton, 1998.

Wustmann, Gustav. *Bilderbuch aus der Geschichte der Stadt Leipzig für Alt und Jung.* Leipzig: Zieger, 1897.

Zerbe, Doreen. *800 Jahre St. Thomas zu Leipzig.* Evangelische Verlagsanstalt, 2014.

Schedule of Church Services in Leipzig

"Der Gottesdienst in Leipzig im 18. Jahrhundert." https://www.sbg.ac.at/pth/texte/30-jahre/leipzig.htm. Institut für Praktische Theologie, Salzburg. Accessed April 2017.
This detailed paper from the Institute for Practical Theology in Salzburg is the source of the Leipzig church schedule on page 12.

Anna Magdalena Bach

* Hübner, Maria, and Hans-Joachim Schulze. *Anna Magdalena Bach: Ein Leben in Dokumenten und Bildern*. Leipzig: Evangelische Verlag-Anst., 2004.

Anna Magdalena's life is difficult to document with any substance. She left no portrait or personal writings, just a paper trail of documents, civic notices, receipts, and other mundane things. Musicologist Maria Hubner has brilliantly compiled and annotated every known document about or concerning Anna Magdalena Bach during and after her life. For those interested in the Bach family, this is a milestone book.

Daily Life

* Camporesi, Piero. *Exotic Brew: The Art of Living in the Age of Enlightenm*ent. Cambridge: Polity, 1994.

* Dülmen, Andrea Van. *Frauenleben im 18. Jahrhundert*. München: Beck, 1992.

Lighting

* Brox, Jane. *Brilliant: The Evolution of Artificial Light*. Boston: Houghton Mifflin Harcourt, 2010.

* Ekirch, A. Roger. *At Day's Close: Night in Times Pa*st. New York: Norton, 2005.

* Koslofsky, Craig. *Evening's Empire: A History of the Night in Early Modern Europe*. Cambridge: Cambridge UP, 2011.

* Thwing, Leroy Livingstone. *Flickering Flames: a History of Domestic Lighting through the Age*s. Rutland, VT: Published for the Rushlight Club, C.E. Tuttle, 1958.

* Matz, Jutta. *Vom Kienspan Zum Laserstrahl: Zur Geschichte der Beleuchtung von der Antike bis Heute*. Husum: Husum Dr.- und Verl.-Ges., 2000.

Clothing

* Bernier, Olivier. *The Eighteenth-century W*oman. Garden City, NY: Doubleday, 1981.

Cunnington, C. Willett., and Cunnington, Phillis. *The History of Underclothes*. London: Faber, 1981.

Hart, Avril, Susan North, Richard Davis, and Leonie Davis. *Seventeenth and Eighteenth-century Fashion in Detail*. London: V & A Pub., 2009.

Kalman, Bobbie. *18th Century Clothing*. New York: Crabtree Pub., 1993.

Eating and table customs

Breunlich, Maria, and Helga Haas. *Karpfen, Krebs und Kälbernes: Ein Bürgerliches Kochbuch aus der Barockzeit*. Wien: Mandelbaum, 2004.

* "Food Timeline." *Food Timeline Website*. Foodtimeline.org, n.d. Web. 20 Sept. 2015. <http://www.foodtimeline.org/index.html>

* Corvinus, Gottlieb Siegmund. *Nutzbares, galantes und curiöses Frauenzimmer-Lexicon*. Leipzig: Johann Friedrich Gleditschs, 1715. Digitized versions available at www.deutschestextarchiv.de and www.diglib.hab.de/drucke/ae-12/start.htm.

* Heise, Ulla. *Kaffee Und Kaffeehaus: Eine Geschichte Des Kaffees*. Frankfurt am Main: Insel, 2002.

Edited by Kiple, Kenneth F. and Ornelas, Kriemhild Conee, eds. *The Cambridge World History of Food: In Two Volumes*. NY: Cambridge UP, 2000.

* Schulze, Hans-Joachim. *Ey! Wie Schmeckt der Coffee Süße: Johann Sebastian Bachs Kaffee-Kantate*. Leipzig: Evang. Verl.-Anst., 2005.

Hygiene

* Ashenburg, Katherine. *The Dirt on Clean: An Unsanitized History*. New York: North Point, 2007.
  The definitive work in English on this subject. If you read one book on the fascinating history of personal hygiene, make it this one.

Böhme, Hartmut. *Kulturgeschichte des Wassers*. Frankfurt Am Main: Suhrkamp, 1988.

* Jungblut, Marie-Paule. *Sei Sauber!: Eine Geschichte der Hygiene und öffentlichen Gesundheitsvorsorge in Europa*. Köln: Wienand, 2004.

* Vigarello, Georges. *Wasser und Seife, Puder und Parfüm: Geschichte der Körperhygiene seit dem Mittelalter*. Frankfurt: Campus, 1988.

Bathing

* Bonneville, Françoise De., and Jane Brenton. *The Book of the Bath*. London: Thames and Hudson, 1998.

Martin, Alfred. *Deutsches Badewesen in vergangenen Tagen: Nebst einem Beitrage zur Geschichte der Deutschen Wasserheilkunde*. Jena: Diederichs, 1906.

Matheus, Michael. *Badeorte und Bäderreisen in Antike, Mittelalter und Neuzeit*. Stuttgart: Franz Steiner, 2001.

Weber, Marga. *Antike Badekultur*. München: Beck, 1996.

Medicine

* Lindemann, Mary. *Medicine and Society in Early Modern Europe*. Cambridge, UK: Cambridge UP, 1999.

* Wynbrandt, James. *The Excruciating History of Dentistry: Toothsome Tales & Oral Oddities from Babylon to Braces*. New York: St. Martin's, 1998.

Women's Health

Hering, Sabine, and Gudrun Maierhof. *Die Unpässliche Frau: Sozialgeschichte der Menstruation und Hygiene*. Pfaffenweiler: Centaurus-Verl.-Ges., 1991.

* Shorter, Edward. *A History of Women's Bodies*. New York: Basic, 1982.

Hair

Cleave, Kendra Van. *18th Century Hair & Wig Styling: History & Step-by-step Techniques*. United States: S.n., 2014.

* Corson, Richard. *Fashions in Hair; the First Five Thousand Years*. New York: Hastings House, 1965.

Princess Elizabeth-Charlotte's Letters

Princess Elizabeth-Charlotte of Bavaria, Duchess of Orleans (1652–1722), also known as Liselotte von der Pfalz, was a German noblewoman who married the brother of King Louis XIV of France in 1688. Until her death in 1722, she wrote countless fascinating letters to her friends and family back home in Germany. This vast correspondence is filled with endless details of royal gossip, palace intrigue, politics, and complaints about the French. Available in print and in online archives.

Bach Resources Online

J. S. Bach Home Page by Jan Hanford and Jan Koster. Excellent portal. www.jsbach.org/

The Bach Cantatas Website. Comprehensive site covering all aspects of Bach's cantatas, other vocal works, and many instrumental works. www.bach-cantatas.com/

Peter Bach, a descendant of J.S. Bach, maintains an informative website. www.bachonbach.com/

BWV Catalog. www.bachcentral.com/BWV/BWV.html

Yo Tomita's excellent Bach bibliography. www.homepages.bw.edu/bachbib/

[All accessed May 2017]

About the Author

Described by the Washington *Post* as *"a model of style and charm, and an irresistible performer,"* tenor David Gordon has forged a versatile international career as singer, teacher, lecturer, and recording artist. He has won critical acclaim as guest soloist with virtually every major North American symphony orchestra, and with other prestigious orchestras, operas, and music festivals on four continents.

Hailed by the St. Louis *Post-Dispatch* as *"one of the greatest interpreters of the Evangelist of our time,"* David is especially known for his vivid and stylish performance of Bach's music for tenor. As a Bach soloist, he has been featured in hundreds of concerts throughout North America, Europe, and Japan with conductors including Robert Shaw, Helmuth Rilling, Bruno Weil, Christopher Hogwood, Greg Funfgeld, David Zinman, Simon Preston, Blanche Honegger Moyse, Fritz Weisse, Richard Westenburg, and Peter Schreier.

On the international operatic stage, David has portrayed 60 principal roles with the San Francisco Opera, Lyric Opera of Chicago, Metropolitan Opera, Houston Grand Opera, Washington National Opera (Kennedy Center), Hamburg Staatsoper, and other stages worldwide. His operatic repertoire includes Monteverdi, Handel, Haydn, Mozart, Rossini, Donizetti, Smetana, Wagner, Mussorgsky, Leoncavallo, Verdi, Puccini, Richard Strauss, Stravinsky, and several world premieres.

A prolific recording artist, David appears on 15 classical CDs for RCA, BMG, Telarc, Decca, and other major labels, in eight centuries of repertoire.

David is also a popular lecturer and master class presenter, and has been a voice instructor at Sonoma State University and the University of California at Berkeley.

David was a central and popular figure at the Carmel Bach Festival in California for more than three decades. He appeared there there as tenor soloist, dramaturge, lecturer, translator, concert narrator, and director of the Festival's Adams Vocal Master Class for young professionals. 2018 was his 30th and final Festival season.

In 2014, David published *Carmel Impresarios,* a major cultural biography of the two visionary women who founded the Carmel Bach Festival and helped establish Carmel-by-the-Sea as an artistic and cultural hotspot in the 1920s and 1930s. The 400-page volume offers a detailed history of theater and music in one of California's most unique regions, and includes nearly 300 vintage illustrations, extensive footnotes, and a detailed appendix and index. Available from any bookseller worldwide. For more information, please visit www.luckyvalleypress.com.

David can be contacted through his website: www.spiritsound.com.

IMAGE SOURCES:

The internet and the digitization of historic material have allowed archived or previously unavailable images to be accessible to all researchers worldwide. Many of the illustrations in this book are derived from image files in the Public Domain acquired from online archives. *See page 134, Further Reading.*

Wikimedia Commons:
Cover, 9, 11, 14, 16, 18, 21, 22, 24, 28, 31, 32, 34, 35, 43, 54, 56, 64, 69, 71, 88, 94, 95, 98, 100, 106, 118. (commons.wikimedia.org)

Library of Congress:
38. (www.loc.gov/collections/)

The Internet Archive:
3, 40, 112, 128. (www.archive.org)

Stock Photos:
Front and rear flyleaves, 11, 25, 78, 87, 109, 114.
(www.123rf.com, www.shutterstock.com)

THE AUTHOR'S COLLECTION:
11, 19, 29, 42, 47, 52, 53, 59, 60, 61, 62, 63, 65, 66, 77, 90, 92, 96, 102.

The maps on Pages 116–117, the Monogram Puzzle on page 81, and the Bach Crown Monogram used throughout this book are original artwork © 2017 David Gordon.

Photograph of the author on page 138 by Rudolf Schroeter.

The Katherine Anne Porter quote shown on page 113 is taken from her introduction to the 1940 Modern Library edition of *Flowering Judas and Other Stories.*

Titles, headers, and display text are set in the Fell Types, late-17th Century type digitally reproduced by Igino Marini.
www.iginomarini.com
Body text composed in Minion

6.20

Index

On the opposite page: A recent photo of the nave of the St. Thomas Church in Leipzig, looking east toward the altar and Bach's grave. The balconies and seating layout have changed greatly since the 1700s.

A detailed photograph of the altar and grave is shown on the opening flyleaf of this book. The exterior of the east end of St. Thomas is shown in the vintage engraving on the cover and in the modern photo on page 78.

St. Thomas today can accommodate more than 1,500 worshippers, and Leipzig's other main church, St. Nicholas, is even larger. These two churches were Bach's workplace for 27 years, and where his great choral masterpieces and hundreds of cantatas were first heard.

CPSIA information can be obtained
at www.ICGtesting.com
Printed in the USA
BVHW041034140121
597841BV00006B/208